PRAISE FOR “SH ..., GREAT THINGS HAPPEN IN THE SILENCE”

"I have had the honor and privilege of knowing Cathy Mott since 2005. For the first half of this relationship, we worked in the same business unit, where I had a chance, almost daily, to witness her unique ability to interact with people. We have both gone onto other roles for the second phase of our relationship. During this time, I've been fortunate to be able to call on her expertise as a coach on several occasions to help other executives grow their own potential and leadership abilities.

One of the most incredible of her many talents is her emotional intelligence. Like many astute executives, she is able to pick up on cues provided by the people around her. However, unlike most people, she has demonstrated an uncanny sense of understanding of what people are feeling and smoothly turns this into getting those people into their "best place" to share, to learn and to grow. She has been able to turn what some people might refer to as "Empathic Ability" into an incredible asset in developing relationships and creating the "safe space" necessary for people to allow themselves to be vulnerable enough to be open to introspection, options, and change.

I am excited to see this book as an opportunity for her to share her secrets with the rest of us on how to develop and enhance our own emotional intelligence."

Don Bignotti, MD, Chief Clinical Officer
Ascension Health

"I have served with Cathy Mott on the ICF Board of Directors, Michigan chapter for three years. Her leadership style is a force to be reckoned with! She brings a wealth of experience to our team and her knowledge is heightened by her high level of Emotional Intelligence. She is always able to sense what our members need as coaches and offer creative solutions. I'm so excited that she is writing this book about Emotional Intelligence and sharing her gifts and talents with the rest of the world."

Jackie Browning, Madame President
ICF Michigan Board of Directors 2019

"As a leader in the field of Human Resources, Talent/Succession, Organizational Development, Coaching, and Performance Management for over 30 years, I can say that Cathy is a uniquely gifted Coach, Facilitator, and Emotional Intelligence professional. I've often referred to her as the "Yoda of Coaching." The easily digestible short stories included in Cathy's book allows you to walk with her and experience each emotion as she did, and then to explore and experience the emotion through your own lens in a safe space and on your own terms. As you make this journey with Cathy, you can feel yourself become part of her stories. You become keenly aware of your emotions and how to "respond" with emotional intelligence, versus just "reacting." Her vulnerability and invitation to you as the reader, to walk in the emotion with her, and evaluate and explore your own emotions, will undoubtedly help you to successfully navigate this journey called "life," as Cathy is a very talented archeologist of the heart, mind, and soul."

Michelle Gill
People & Organization Strategist & Adjunct Professor
Michigan State University, Broad College of Business

"Cathy is a great leader and executive coach. Her unique gifts allow her to get beneath the surface and identify the true needs of her high achieving clients. She has worked with several of my leaders and improved their effectiveness both personally and professionally. Her ability to listen and connect while remaining objective is a gift. She is very effective in helping individuals focus on what really matters. She brings great insight into every encounter. I would recommend her without reservation."

Charles E. Sanders, Jr., MD, FACP, Retired Vice
President of Medical Education and Research

"Cathy seized her training with us with a passion and energy that was inspiring not only to the instructors, but the other students in the class. Her insights and coaching expertise shone brightly as she shared her experiences and viewpoints on all aspects of emotional intelligence. Her passion for learning and helping others grow is evident in everything she does. We're proud to call her one of our Social + Emotional Intelligence Coaches and are eager to see how this book launch will lead her toward future successes."

Amy Sargent, Executive Director
Institute for Social + Emotional Intelligence

Great Things Happen in the Silence

Shh... JUST LISTEN!

CATHY MOTT

Definitions of emotions are taken from:
Merriam-Webster's Dictionary
Dictionary.com

Scripture quotations are taken from:
The New World Translation of the Holy Scriptures

ISBN 978-1-5323-9917-6

Published by:
CWC Leadership Development, LLC
www.cwcleadershipdevelopment.com

Cover & Interior Design by LaTanya Orr, Selah XL

Printed and bound in the United States of America

DEDICATION

I dedicate this book to my loving husband of 36 years (yes 36 years), Tony Mott, who has been so supportive to me on this journey. On the days when I wanted to stop writing and give up, he was always there with the appropriate nudge that I needed to continue. Then there were the days when I said, "Who am I fooling? No one is going to want to read this book." He was there with the right words at the right time. He listened to many of the stories in the book and would give me feedback. He would tell me how much he loved many of the stories, because they each had a story within a story, or he would simply shake his head and say, "That's deep...You're deep!" For all of the right words at the right time, your patience and loving support, I say, thank you, Honey...I love you!

I also, dedicate this book to my three children for being bold, brave and fearless in the face of tragedy. The courage each of you demonstrate, ignites a fire in my belly, warms my heart and soul and compels me to pull my shoulders back, hold my head high and say with great pride, "Those are MY babies!" Thank you for allowing me to share a piece of your lives in this book and for allowing me to have a seat in your audience as I watch you perform this thing called life.

Thank you Tonysha, TJ & Jasmine

I would not be here without my fabulous parents. I also dedicate this book to my Mom and Dad for giving me such a firm foundation and a happy childhood. You both made me feel so secure and so special that I would grow up to walk through life with a positive outlook and an emboldened level of confidence. You both believed in me, made me feel adored in your presence, and consistently told me I could be anything I wanted to be. It was growing up in this firm foundation and because of your love and support, that I have surpassed my own dreams. Even though my mom is not here to read this book I take great solace in knowing that she would be so proud of me (her baby.)

Thank you, Momma and Daddy

ACKNOWLEDGMENTS

"Standing on the Shoulders of Giants." (Isaac Newton)

Many of us grew up listening to or reading stories about giants. A few that come to my mind are *Goliath, The Jolly Green Giant, Gulliver* and of course the giant from the *"Jack and the Beanstalk."* All of them were known for their large stature and strength. I would like an opportunity to acknowledge just a few giants in my professional career that have allowed me to stand on their shoulders without wobbling because of the strength of their leadership and moral character. These individuals left a road-map for me to follow even after they were no longer present in my daily life. I'm happy to say that I am still connected to each and every one of them and would like to take this opportunity to acknowledge them.

Toni Flowers: Thank you Toni for always taking the time to hold up the "mirror", and invite me ever so gently to look into it. Our conversations had a profound effect on me, your use of word pictures and your ability to give feedback created the space for me to begin the journey of discovering my God given gifts and talents. You were the one that said, "I think you would be a great facilitator." I never saw that in myself, but you did! Well, look at how that one statement would go on to define a large part of my life. When we worked together, thank you for always asking, "How is Cathy feeling today?" I loved that question, however, I was even more pleased when you told me why you always asked that question, because you knew if I was feeling good, you would get my best work. I love it! Thank you Toni Flowers for being YOU!

Denise Brooks-Williams: Thank you Denise for being a powerful representation of a woman in leadership and at the same time fully involved in raising your children and being present in your family life. I always marveled at how you were able to do both. I also admired your calm, confident demeanor in the midst of a crisis. No matter how many projects we were juggling at one time, you were consistently able to strategically find solutions. Your steadiness provided security for me which allowed me to blossom under your leadership. Thank YOU for your example.

Michelle Gill: Thank you Michelle for our glorious and memorable 10-10-10 walk that we shared in our executive coach training. This walk changed our lives and our relationship has been such a blessing in my life ever since that fall day in 2013. You have inspired me to use my gifts in so many ways and have also provided opportunities for me to stretch and grow as a leader. I think one of the most important things you've taught me is how to introduce myself to an audience. The first time I heard you introduce me to a group, I wanted to meet me! LOL I have since adjusted my intros to include some of the things I often forget to mention. Thank YOU for introducing me to myself. I'm forever grateful for your example of leadership.

Don Bignotti: Thank you Don for the many years of providing me the opportunity to see emotional intelligence in action. I've had the privilege of observing you in the role of physician and an administrator. I remember many days watching you come out of a meeting that was strategically focused that dealt with facts and figures, however, you were able to immediately shift to interact compassionately with your patients. I've always admired that about you. More recently I would like to thank you for allowing me the privilege to partner with you as we continue to work together to inspire, support and provide resources for leaders to walk in their greatness. I appreciate YOU!

Pat Barlow: Thank you Pat for seeing me as I truly am. I would even venture to say, you saw through me. You have coached me verbally and silently by your example. I want to thank you for asking powerful questions that literally changed the trajectory of my life for the better. However, I'm most grateful to you because you helped me put a name to my ability to be able feel what other people feel. I'll never forget the day when you said, "You're empathic." I didn't know what it meant, but I have read and researched just about everything there is to know about it. I have been able to educate myself and learn how to use this gift. Thank you Pat for being YOU!

TABLE OF CONTENTS

Foreword	xi
Introduction	xiii
How to Use this Book	xix
Disclaimer	xxi
The EQ Quadrant	xxii
What is Emotional Intelligence?	xxiii
Emotions	
Anger	1
Anguish	7
Authentic	15
Blessed	21
Confident	29
Connected	35
Courage	41
Defeated	49
Depressed	55
Ecstasy	63
Excited	69
Fear	75
Gifted	81
Gratitude	87
Grief	95
Guilt	101
Happy	107
Inadequate	113
Insightful	119
Jealousy	125
Love	131
Numb	143
Nurtured	149
Offended	155
Sad	161
Special	167
Squashed	171
Tired	179
Validated	185
Vulnerable	193

List of Emotions 199
Additional Journal Pages 200
EQ Leadership Training Questions 207
Book Club Questions 211
Letter to the Reader 213
About the Author 215

FOREWORD

Daily, we are bombarded with noises that present themselves in various ways from multiple sources. Each noise has an impact on us mentally, spiritually, physically or emotionally. For this writing, I will define noise as sounds that attract attention and send a message. The first noise of the day may begin with the sound of the alarm clock awakening us from a restful sleep. That awakening sound may be an annoying buzz, a few bars of your favorite song or even the tranquil sound of a waterfall. It doesn't matter which sound has been chosen for your alarm, all those sounds communicate the message that the time of awakening has come.

In her book, *Shh…Just Listen! Great Things Happen in the Silence*, Cathy Mott invites her readers to consider embarking upon a personal journey into the silence. She takes the mystery out of the traverse by informing us that "great things" are ahead. She further cautions her readers that there is a requirement to obtain those great things…listening.

We are not invited to take this personal journey to a destination not frequently traveled without the benefit of a guide. Cathy has cut down the brush and blazed a trail ahead of her travelers. She has deeply explored, defined and shared her own personal journeys into her silence and generously allowed us to take part in her experiences and learn from her listening.

I have had the great pleasure of knowing Cathy Mott for many years and I am very confident in identifying her as one of the most "internally in-tune" people I know. Through the years, I have witnessed her run the gamut of emotions, ranging from the highest joys of a new addition to her family to the deepest sorrow of the loss of a parent and many other emotions in between. I assure you that she is introspective, self-aware and courageous in her venture into this avenue of emotional transparency.

Several years ago, Cathy reported to me at our workplace. My daily habit was to assess the productivity status of my team. I asked everyone, except Cathy, "How are you today?" My question for Cathy was always, "How are you feeling today?" Once, Cathy asked me, "Why do you always ask me how I'm feeling?" My response was, "If you're not feeling good, you won't produce well. However, if you feel good and are flying high, I can expect your best work!" The emotional well being of your team should matter to every leader. High emotional wellbeing = high productivity!

When you reflect on your personal foray into emotional growth and development and are pleased with how far you have come on the journey to emotional wellness...you want to share the trip with others. One might ask, "why raise the blinds and allow the world to peek into the window of your emotions?" When you possess high emotional intelligence, you have acquired the skill that is said to be the greatest predictor of professional success. Emotional Intelligence (EI) enables individuals to gain insight into how their choices and behaviors impact themselves and those around them.

Consider this book as a mental collection of souvenirs, a virtual photo album or scrapbook of emotional awareness. Cathy has shared her experiences with her emotions and detailed their impact on her well-being. Think of it as a road-map to guide you on your own journey of exploration and self-discovery. Allow yourself time for deep contemplation. Quiet the noise during your time with this book. I have it on great authority that...*Great Things Happen in The Silence...Shh...Just Listen!*

Dr. Toni Flowers
Vice President & Chief Diversity
& Inclusion Officer
Roper St. Francis Healthcare

INTRODUCTION

My name is Cathy Mott and I am passionate about emotions and Emotional Intelligence (EI). This passion serves me well as an Executive/Leadership Coach and as a Certified Social and Emotional Intelligence Coach and Trainer. I've had the distinct pleasure of training over 7,000 individuals on a national and international level. I've also been honored to coach/train hundreds of leaders in different industries, Automotive (Mercedes Benz Financial Services); Education (Michigan State University), Healthcare (Trinity Health), just to name a few, which has allowed me to have a multifaceted look at the value of Emotional Intelligence (EI) and how it is a necessary component for successful leaders today. I believe they are the very foundation for any successful and rewarding relationship both personally and professionally. I have discovered through my own personal and professional journey the tremendous value of being able to sit silently, listen and validate my own emotions. Nevertheless, it takes strength and courage to walk this journey; courage to be still when it hurts and strength to exercise self-control amid emotions that cause internal combustion. All of these elements are needed to develop and increase our emotional intelligence which is a crucial skill needed for successful leadership. One of my core beliefs is that we are all leaders in our own lives, so this journey is open for anyone who is bold enough to embark upon this exploration.

Let's talk a little bit about Emotional Intelligence (EI). Here is the dictionary's definition:

"Skill in perceiving, understanding and managing emotions and feelings." (dictionary.com)

Emotional Intelligence involves four components: *Self-Awareness, Self-Management, Awareness of Others and Social Management.* Here is my personal definition of these four quadrants in action; "being able to experience an emotion in the moment; name it; have an awareness of why you're feeling that way and then validate that emotion; and because you are keenly aware of your own emotions you have an awareness of what is going on with others in the moment. With all of this EI knowledge, you can make an informed decision to respond to a particular social setting instead of reacting. Whew! That's a mouthful, right? However, people with high EI can often do this in a matter of seconds. Therefore, they typically are some of the best leaders within organizations whether they have an official leadership title or not. They have the ability to inspire others to follow them regardless of where they are on the organizational chart. Dr. Toni Flowers, (my former boss) used such a vivid word picture to describe emotional intelligence in action, and I have never forgotten it. She used to always say, "If you're a leader and no one is following you, you're just taking a walk." Can't you mentally see that? Leaders who inspire others to follow, often without asking, are responsive in stressful situations instead of reactive. They are also intentional at building effective relationships because they are aware of what's going on with others and are better equipped to manage social settings.

Let's explore the difference between responding and reacting. Responding is an intentional choice made with self-control, empathy, and discernment, which can result in personal and professional growth and assist in yielding the results you desire. Reacting, however, can be impulsive without self-control that can lead to the vicious cycle of unwanted behaviors and regret. I have coached hundreds of leaders who noticed a huge improvement in their ability to lead their teams effectively when their behavior shifted from reactive to responsive in their leadership acumen.

It's been said that, "EQ is four times more important in determining the success of an individual than IQ." (Daniel Goleman). How profound! However, in my work of training and facilitating, I have discovered that for many people their first exposure to EI is in a leadership development training class. Participants in these classes range in age anywhere from the mid-30s to early 60s and at least 75 percent of them say, "I wish I had known about EI when I was much younger." I usually will ask, "When?" They always say, "High school or definitely before entering college." My preference would be high school students because they begin to experience a rush of new emotions and tend to isolate themselves from their parents and adults in general and only hang with their peers who are themselves riding the same emotional roller coaster. I know, I digress…just another one of my passions. (Teaching EI to high school students.)

In my Emotional Intelligence training course, I typically facilitate an exercise where I ask the participants to pull out a blank sheet of paper; I give them 90 seconds to write down as many emotions as they can think of in that time frame. Remember, I have trained thousands, and the majority of participants can usually name no more than four to six emotions. I've had two individuals name up to seventeen. They were "rockstars," to all of the other participants who thought their abilities were astounding. Given the same assignment, how many emotions do you think you could name in 90 seconds? Have you ever thought about how many emotions exist? I'm not going to give you a number because I want you to explore, research and discover a plethora of emotions; I'm sure you will be amazed at what you will unearth.

I take great pride in working with my clients and creating a space for them to discover and articulate emotions that have been lingering internally for years. So often these emotions have been repressed, silenced and certainly never validated, for many of them remain nameless. They have been harnessed internally only to create physical manifestations in the body that can sometimes take our attention away from what's going on emotionally. I believe all emotions manifest themselves somewhere in the physical body.

My tagline as a coach is, *"I specialize in introducing people to themselves."* Some time ago, I recognized that I could not do for others what I had not done for myself. So about 20 years ago, I created a space for me to come face-to-face with who I really am. My physical manifestation of the emotions that were repressed and muzzled inside of me lead to a diagnosis of lupus and depression. Yes, the big "D." This process was scary and painful, but if I had a chance to do it all over again, I would intentionally choose to do it sooner. I wish I had the knowledge, understanding, and courage to begin this process voluntarily instead of being pushed into the dark hole of depression, feeling as if I had no choice. I felt alone and powerless, even though I had been happily married for 15 years with three children. On the outside looking in, my life looked great. However, the person on the inside of me was screaming, "What about me?!" She was angry and would not be silenced any longer! She demanded a face-to-face meeting with the person I presented to the world. I knew I had to stop and take time to "Shh…Just listen" to her. This introduction to myself was not on my terms, but I knew I could no longer deny her request for she had made me physically weak, powerless and feeling hopeless. I had no idea that this would be the beginning of my journey to increasing my emotional intelligence.

A huge help for me on my quest to become more emotionally attentive to what was going on inside of me was journaling. This is where great things begin to happen in the silence. I started 20 years ago and I haven't stopped. My goal for this book is to create a space for you, the reader, to capture and unleash your emotions on your terms. I will share some of my deepest emotions with you, and we will walk through elements of emotional intelligence together. I will define the emotion, and then share my experience and/or time spent with this emotion. I have also entertained questions that have helped me tremendously on this exploration: "If faced with this situation again, what would I do differently? What are the lessons learned from listening to each particular emotion? As you will discover, I will then sit quietly and shh…just listen to the value of each emotion and capture the lesson learned in writing. There is something so powerful and therapeutic in writing. I would even venture to say, that with some of my stories, it proved to be cathartic.

I know for many of you journaling will not be easy, yes it will be a struggle. Let me share just some of the many benefits of journaling, with a targeted focus on the benefits related to emotional intelligence. Studies show there is an "emotional release that comes from journaling which lowers stress and anxiety and promotes better sleep. Journaling also helps you to express yourself and increases your awareness of self and others. Since expressive writing helps you to process your thoughts and emotions, it's no surprise that it also helps to boost your immune system and attain greater peace and calm." (Matthew Kulley - How keeping a journal can change your life.) I have also noticed a significant difference in my clients who journal and those who do not. My clients who practice journaling tend to make behavioral changes and reach their goals at a faster pace than those who do not to journal.

My personal journey, along with the experiences I have shared with the thousands I have coached and/or for those with whom I facilitated a training course, has compelled me to develop this 30-day workbook focused on increasing your emotional awareness. It is my desire to create a space for you to give a voice to and listen to your emotions. It is also my hope that this workbook will appeal to both men and women. I know many women will enjoy this process, but as a coach, I have consistently created a safe space for my male clients as well. In this quiet space, men have shed tears, bowed low in their body language and have come face-to-to face with themselves for the very first time. Many have permitted themselves to move out of their head and into their hearts. Some have confessed uncertainty, fear, shame, and guilt. However, because of this safe space of no judgment, these same men will often rise up and stand tall because they have unleashed heavy emotions that have weighed them down for years. They are now better equipped to recognize a larger span of emotions in others because they have now experienced a broader range of emotion themselves. They indeed have become better leaders, fathers, husbands, sons, brothers, friends and colleagues.

With this Emotional Intelligence workbook, I've created a road-map for you to capture your experience with each emotion I've written about (or a similar emotion) on the subsequent pages. I have also included a few blank pages in the back of the book for you to explore and listen to emotions that I have not written about. This is your journey! My goal is to simply create the space to capture these emotions, live in the moment with them and shh… just listen to the value they can bring and learn the lesson. Keep in mind as you write, this should be a place of non-judgment and validation. Remember emotions are not good or bad, they just are. It's how we respond to them that determines the value placed on our emotions. Give yourself, time, space and permission to take this journey…no passport needed. Commit with an open mind and an open heart. In some respects, I'll be there with you all the way. Shh…Just Listen...you'll hear me because, "Great Things Happen in the Silence."

HOW TO USE THIS BOOK

Life is full of noise and distractions, with no time for solace or self-discovery. If you take a look at the cover of this book, my goal is for the reader to be intentional about taking time to listen to the internal dialogue that happens within us almost every minute of every day. Just think, what if you're in a relationship with someone who never listens to you? How would you feel about that person and/or the relationship? Angry, frustrated, misunderstood, taken for granted, or maybe feeling like you're not important enough for that person to listen to you.

My life experience has proven to me that the person we're in a relationship with who is not being heard, is ourselves. Many of us, myself included, have walked around for years not listening to our emotions and have chosen to ignore them. Then there are the emotions that refuse to be ignored and so they remain quiet or lie dormant in the body, only to manifest themselves as a physical ailment as time goes by.

We've taken this course because sometimes we feel our emotions have no value or we do not have a safe space to explore them without interruption or judgment. My desire is that you, the reader, take the time to Shh…Just Listen and marvel at the great things that can happen in the silence.

I have written about 30 different emotions and my personal experience with each of them. On the subsequent page, I have created a space for you to write about your personal experience with each emotion or one that is similar. I have found that there is insurmountable value and wisdom while exploring the story behind each emotion. I have also examined my thoughts, feelings, and reactions surrounding each emotion. I learned when I was in school for executive coaching, that tears are valuable and that everyone has a story to tell. Sometimes in my moment of silence, it creates a conduit for tears that have been trapped inside.

I'm hoping you will commit to a 30-day transformational journey with me. I am inviting you to create the time and the space to give voice to unheard emotions and feelings that find themselves locked inside, secretly manifesting themselves as physical ailments just to get your attention. Be intentional about the space you create for yourself, grab your favorite cup of coffee or tea, an ink pen and create the space for this 30-day transformation as you slow down and take the time to Shh…Just Listen.

DISCLAIMER

This book is not intended as a substitute for the medical advice of physicians. The reader should regularly consult a physician in matters relating to his/her mental and physical health particularly with respect to feelings or thoughts that may require diagnosis and/or medical attention from a physician.

In addition, the author and publisher have made every effort to ensure that the information in this book was correct at press time. The author and publisher do not assume and hereby disclaim any liability or loss arising in any way whatsoever.

THE EQ QUADRANT

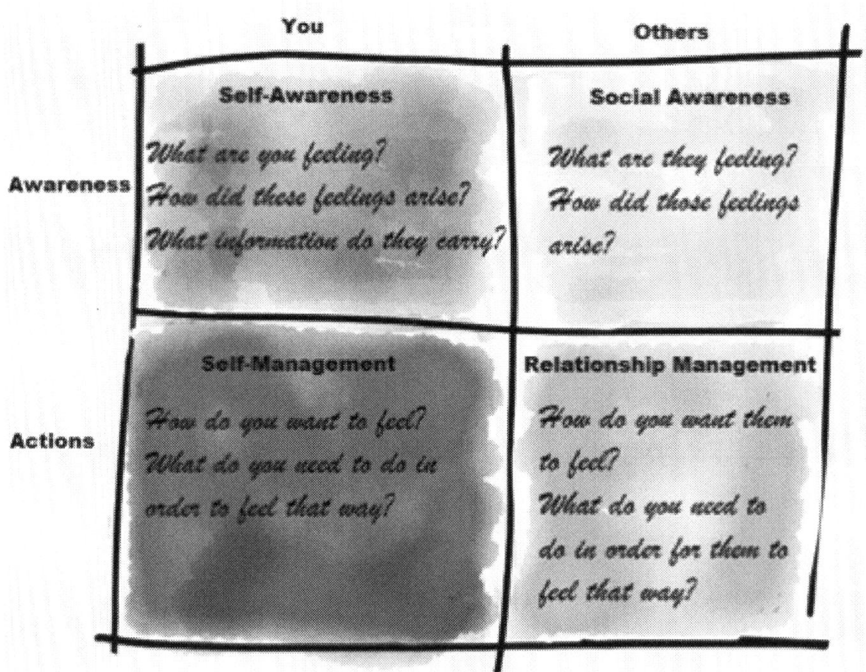

Copyright: Picture taken from the "Coach with the Green Hat"

EMOTIONAL INTELLIGENCE (EI)

is an individual's capability —

- To recognize their own, and other people's emotions,
- To discriminate between different feelings and label them appropriately,
- To use emotional information to guide thinking and behavior, and
- To manage and/or adjust emotions to adapt environments or achieve one's goal(s).

EMOTIONAL QUOTIENT (EQ)

is how one measures Emotional Intelligence.

EMOTIONS

ANGER

Anger – "A strong feeling of displeasure and usually of antagonism."

- Merriam-Webster's Dictionary

MY EXPERIENCE WITH THIS EMOTION:

This day started out beautifully. I've engaged in my "bucket filling" morning routine and I'm excited. I'm facilitating one of my favorite courses - "Leader as Coach" with a great group of participants and things are going well.

It's time for our first 15-minute break, and during that time, I check my email. What a mistake!!! I received an email from a client that really made my blood boil. I was angry. This email accused me of not following their corporate policy and several people within the organization were copied on this email. I'm sure most of you have been in a similar situation. To me, this was an attack against my integrity and my character. Indeed I am in the emotion of anger. Everything inside of me wanted to respond in defense, "How dare you!...Who do you think you are?!" In that moment, I even started typing out a response in the heat of anger.

HOW DID I MANAGE THIS EMOTION?

I remembered the 24-hour rule on responding to emails that upset you. I also asked myself a question: "How do you want this to turn out?" My response to that question: "I want to use the leadership tools and techniques that I teach to others, and I want to handle this in a way that would make me feel proud of my behavior and would add to my character and reputation as a Leader and Coach.

I learned through teaching "Crucial Conversations" that questions are powerful when our emotions are trying to hijack us. They help to shift the blood flow from the back of the brain, which is where our emotions emerge to the frontal cortex, which is the more logical portion of the brain so that we can make a more reasonable choice on how to respond instead of reacting to a situation. So what did I do? I closed that email and continued to teach my class for the day. I had my assistant reach out to this person and schedule a video conference. I felt like this was a conversation I needed to have face-to-face.

HOW DID I MANAGE THE SOCIAL SETTING:

The meeting was scheduled a couple of days later. I thought about what I wanted to say and how I would say it. I knew from my training that I needed to start out sharing how I felt when I read the email. I would indeed use the principles from "Crucial Conversations". I even practiced in my head and rehearsed it out loud a couple of times.

So here we are face-to-face. After we exchanged pleasantries, I began. "I wanted to have an opportunity to respond to your email, but I thought we should have a face-to-face conversation. When I read your email, I felt angry, hurt, and scolded. I also felt that as a business owner, my character and integrity were called into question." I also read a statement from her email, and then I invited her into the conversation by asking her, "What are your thoughts?" She immediately apologized profusely.

I also mentioned that we have on several occasions talked about the value of "trust and assuming good intentions" with others and how she had not extended that courtesy to me. She again apologized. My tone of voice was very mild, but firm. We continued our discussion and this person said, "I really messed that up. I should not have sent that email. How can I make it right?" I responded, "Your apology certainly is a great start, but please send an email of apology and copy the same individuals you copied in the first email. I'm thankful she was willing to make it right and that our relationship is intact. I would also say that it's better than it was before this disagreement.

LESSONS LEARNED FROM THIS EMOTION:

Relationships can be strengthened when conflict is handled well. Most relationships are good until there is conflict. The strength of a relationship can be tested when feelings are wounded. Being able to express my feelings and articulate the reasons why was empowering and therapeutic. The emotion of anger typically means that someone has crossed our boundaries. So being able to have a crucial conversation that re-established the boundaries in this business relationship was very rewarding. The biggest lesson for me is that it's so much better to "respond" to anger than react. This is Emotional Intelligence at its best.

IF FACED WITH THIS SITUATION AGAIN, WHAT WOULD I DO DIFFERENTLY:

I would probably handle it the same. The only thing that I have changed since then is that I'm very careful about which emails I read when I'm facilitating a class. I don't want to disrupt my "mojo" while I'm training. That day it took me a couple of hours to get back to where I was internally before I read that email.

My experience with this emotion:

How did I manage this emotion?

How did I manage the social setting?

Lessons learned from this emotion:

If faced with this situation again, what would I do differently:

REFLECTIONS

ANGUISH

Anguish –"Extreme pain, distress, or anxiety."

- Merriam-Webster's Dictionary

MY EXPERIENCE WITH THIS EMOTION:

I remember this emotion well. I was on a business trip in Tennessee preparing to facilitate a leadership development training for a large Auto Parts Manufacturer. I had arrived early to allow myself a day of shopping and a nice meal. I chose Carrabba's as my restaurant of choice, where I still had to wait 20 minutes to get in on a Monday night. I figured the food must be pretty good so I waited. I'm finally seated at a table and order my favorite wine, (Moscato) and place my order. Shortly after, my plate hits the table, my oldest daughter called. I answered the phone and I heard her screaming and crying. I got up from the table and walked out of the restaurant because she was trying to tell me something, but I couldn't hear her or understand. Once outside, I told her to calm down and repeat what she was trying to tell me. She's still crying but I'm in another state. I can't get to her to put my arms around her and calm her down. I again say, "What is it, what is it? Calm down and tell me!"

After a few minutes of crying and sniffling, she was finally able to articulate that her husband had been found dead at their home. I felt as if someone had dropped a boulder on my chest. I felt as if I could not breathe, and my chest could not expand to allow oxygen in. I can't even believe it! I cannot even begin to tell you the range of emotions I felt, but the one I remember the most is sheer anguish. The definition of this word encompasses so many emotions, such as agony, pain, torment, distress, sorrow, grief, and heartache just to name a few. I must have felt all of these emotions in a matter of seconds. I can only comfort her with my words and my tone of voice because of the distance between us. That hardly seemed to be enough. I wanted to put my arms around her and try to soothe her sheer pain and agony. However, I was hundreds of miles away while my daughter was suffering intense pain and trauma.

We talked for quite a while and after she calmed down and tried to wrap her head around this tragedy, she asked me this question: "How am I going to tell the boys?"

She has three sons who absolutely adored their dad. At this time, they were 5, 9, and 11. Deep down inside, I never wanted her to tell them because it's such a life-changing event; it was horrific. I can remember being told that my mom had passed and at that moment I think a little piece of me died on the inside. I wanted so much to spare my grandsons from the same experience. I wanted to protect them from the awful reality of losing their dad. Because of what had just happened to them, their lives would never be the same. There were days when I wished I had not known about my mom's death. Losing a parent can shake your foundation. I wanted so much for their security not to be taken away. I knew once they were told, they would be forever changed. My chest is heavy and my heart still hurts (2 ½ years later) as I write about this emotion of anguish.

HOW DID I MANAGE THIS EMOTION?

Prayer, prayer, and more prayer. I prayed intensely, gathered myself and then called my husband, family, and friends to provide and receive comfort. I even called my girlfriends and asked them to go over to my daughter's house and support her. After this memory, I can't even tell you how I managed this emotion, but I do feel like it was a miracle what happens next.

HOW DID I MANAGE THE SOCIAL SETTING?

I rushed back to my hotel to try and get a flight out that night to go home and be with my family. Unfortunately, there were no flights going out that night. The earliest flight I could get was just an hour before my original flight costing $979.00. So I decided to keep my original flight and facilitate the leadership training I had initially flown to Tennessee to teach.

The training was about functioning as a team, establishing trust and learning to be vulnerable with one another for a group of twelve men. Near the end of the training, each participant had to answer a series of questions about their childhood and personal life challenges that they had to overcome in life. The setting in the room was such that they all had to sit in a circle so that they could see one another. With me, there was thirteen of us sitting in the circle. Their stories were incredible.

The twelve men were from different backgrounds, different cultures, different countries and shared their experiences. Some experiences were sad, shocking and horrific events that happened in their childhood. I felt as though their stories were answering my prayers. A couple of men shared stories about losing their dad at an early age. Another shared the story of losing both parents, growing up hungry and living on the streets after running away from several abusive foster homes. Many of the men began to shed tears and comfort one another in this tender space of vulnerability. I was intentional to be fully present with them in this moment. I was honored to share in this space with them, for hearing their sheer grief and sadness made me recognize that eventually my daughter and my three grandsons would be okay.

At the close of the training, I thanked the group collectively and individually for sharing their stories. I never shared with them what was going on in my life at that moment. I don't think I could have composed myself to finish the training and make it to the airport, if I had.

After the class was over, I hurried, packed my bags and rushed to the airport. I am still in disbelief that I was able to facilitate this training. I think it's called "compartmentalizing". Whatever it is, that's what I did. I arrived at the airport, returned my rental car, and went through the security checkpoint. It's at this moment that I began to fall apart. I sat in the airport and cried and rocked myself back and forth with my arms crossed as if I was giving myself a hug. I guess the reality of everything that had taken place was beginning to set in. Within a matter of moments of walking through the checkpoint, I lost my credit card at the airport. It was just awful. I quickly called the credit card company and the customer service representative asked me "how are you doing tonight?" I told him that I wasn't doing well at all, my son-in-law had just died, and I was trying to make it back home from a business trip. This was the first time I had heard myself say that out loud, and I recognized it was real, and I began to cry. I cried and cried for quite some time as my customer service representative tried to comfort me. He was so patient and kind, just what I needed at that time. I still believe there are great customer service experiences happening every day. I was certainly blessed to have this awesome experience. After talking to him, I was able to pull myself together and eventually board the plane.

LESSONS LEARNED FROM THIS EMOTION:

First off, I would like to add an S and change this to lessonS learned because there were so many. I've learned from this experience and the emotion of anguish that prayer makes us powerful beyond what we could ever imagine. We're so much more capable of what we think we are when we chose to reach beyond our human limitations. The choice not to try to navigate trials and tribulations on our own is a powerful choice that can be made in a weakened state. If someone would have told me that I would have received a call from my daughter with such awful news and afterward I would be able to facilitate a class and fly back the next day I would not have believed it!!! I know for certain that I did not do this on my own strength. I have also learned there is so much value in hearing the life story of others; hearing those twelve men tell their stories touched my heart and soul, and helped me on a small level to begin the healing process. I guess connecting with others and being vulnerable has the power to heal, to incite and to encourage others. Often these conversations are free of charge. All that's required is the intention to buy out the time, create the space, and be courageous enough to open our hearts.

IF FACED WITH THIS SITUATION AGAIN, WHAT WOULD I DO DIFFERENTLY:

I can truly say, I can't answer this question and honestly hope I never have to be faced with this situation like this again. However, I know you're probably wondering how my daughter and her three boys are doing. It's been two and a half years since that awful phone call that brought about such deep anguish. Since then, there have definitely been times of grief, anger, sadness, and disbelief, but overall they are doing better than I would have ever imagined they would be. My daughter is learning how to be a single mom raising three boys and helping them through the grief process. At the same time, she is acutely aware that she needs to process her own grief. She/we have a large support system and to see how so many have rallied around all of us is amazing. Even with all of the love and support we've received, we will still continue to experience anguish as a result of such a great loss to our family and especially my grandsons.

My experience with this emotion:

How did I manage this emotion?

How did I manage the social setting?

Lessons learned from this emotion:

If faced with this situation again, what would I do differently:

REFLECTIONS

AUTHENTIC

Authentic –"True to one's own personality, spirit, or character."

- Merriam-Webster's Dictionary

MY EXPERIENCE WITH THIS EMOTION:

We all have a set of values we live by. Whether we've taken the time to write them down or have experienced the "Value Cards" exercise. (Sixty cards with a different value on each card. Participants are asked to choose six values that closely aligns with who they are and the life they have created for themselves.). Some values were instilled in us as children: Respect, Integrity, Kindness...the list could go on and could be very different for each person. I have a value system that I have lived by for years — fifty percent are childhood family values, fifty percent are my own as I found myself and declared myself "grown."

I won't list them all, but I can genuinely say the values that govern my life are my relationship with God first, family, and I'm a strong advocate of self-care. The self-care piece did not come from my childhood, for I saw my mother work tirelessly for the sake of others, however, she seemed to enjoy it. While I've tried to follow in her footsteps, this is one area where I've intentionally created my own path to follow.

I give you this background because about two years ago I was faced with a situation/opportunity that would be like a dream come true for many people. I had exited corporate America for about a year at this time and I was building a business and trying to find my niche. I did TV and radio, seminars, facilitation, and Executive Coaching. Along this journey, I had the opportunity to be interviewed on *Blog Talk Radio* by Jim Masters and Doug Llewelyn from the "People's Court Television Show." What a great experience!!! Well, a few weeks after my interview with Doug Llewelyn, I received a call from *NBC*...yes *NBC*! I was offered an opportunity to host a reality TV show around life coaching. The goal was to take an "unknown" coach and make them a well-known star. The offer started with flying me to New York, limousine service, and a personal stylist, make-up artist - all the things I love. I love getting dressed up. I'd also be on tour for a year. I listened to the offer with much initial enthusiasm. I was honored and excited beyond belief! However, after hearing the *NBC* representative out, I declined because this offer would have taken me across the country on tour for a year. My decision was based on my values and character. I think it's so powerful to come face-to-face with who you say you are, and who you really are. This was that moment for me where the stakes were extremely high! To answer in the affirmative would take me away from my regular spiritual routine, away from my family and all of the things I love. Some may feel "You can have it all," but as I dwell in this emotion I feel like I already do! I love my life! It allows me to spend much-needed quality time in silence, prayer, and meditation. My family is also very essential to my sense of well being and my definition of success. I value the time I'm able to spend with my hubby of 36 years, my three children, and my eight grandchildren, who I spend time with regularly.. Then there is Thursday date night with my dad. No job or position is as grand as my values and living a life that is authentically me and authentically mine! The emotion of feeling *authentic* comes from living what I say my values are with no regrets. I have created a life "true to my personality, spirit, and character." Six months later, I received a second phone call from *NBC* with the same offer, and the NBC representative says, "The offer is still on the table, are you sure you're not interested?" I gave the same answer - "No." He then said, "Do you think you will be interested in the near future?" I gave the same answer, "No."

HOW DID I MANAGE THIS EMOTION?

Being able to consistently stand in my values and say no is definitely the intense emotion of authenticity. I managed it with integrity, a sense of direction, and knowing what success means to me and not being governed by how most people would define success.

LESSONS LEARNED FROM THIS EMOTION:

Authenticity is a beautiful thing. You can't put a price tag on it, and it can't be purchased. It takes constant effort and intentional growth. Once achieved…it's priceless.

IF FACED WITH THIS SITUATION AGAIN, WHAT WOULD I DO DIFFERENTLY:

I did have that opportunity. I would still say no. I'm three years into Executive Coaching, Consultant, and being a business owner. I'm pleased with the growth of my business and how I've managed to maintain my values and what's important to me.

My experience with this emotion:

How did I manage this emotion?

How did I manage the social setting?

Lessons learned from this emotion:

If faced with this situation again, what would I do differently:

REFLECTIONS

REFLECTIONS

BLESSED

***Blessed* – "*Bringing pleasure, contentment, or good fortune.*"**

- Merriam-Webster's Dictionary

MY EXPERIENCE WITH THIS EMOTION:

I know I've consistently talked about the void of losing my mom. However, I wanted to take the opportunity to share the blessing that has come from this loss - my relationship with my dad.

When my mom was alive, I spent so much time focusing on her and our relationship, and that's typically what mothers and daughters do. She always made me feel so special! "Yes, I'm the baby!" But since her loss, my dad and I have developed a beautiful relationship. It's been five years since my mom passed and I've learned so much about him. I have reflected back on all of the things that I thought were just a regular routine with my dad, like putting on his black tuxedo and picking up his trumpet, putting on his nice hat and walking out of the house. I'll explain how this applies later. These days I'm just so impressed with him. I have always viewed him as a distinguished man, always somewhere sitting with his legs crossed and able to carry on a conversation with anyone about anything. (My 11-year-old grandson, Anthony has these same gifts.)

I will share just a few things that I've learned about him in the past five years. My dad was a trumpet player for Motown. He played with the most famous groups - The Temptations, Diana Ross and The Supremes, Sammy Davis Jr., The Four Tops, and many more. These things I knew, but the time we spend together now, would provide more depth and brevity to what I already knew. Like this story, I never knew he played the show where Diana Ross introduced Michael Jackson and The Jackson 5. I also recently found out that he was actually at Hitsville Motown in Detroit when Stevie Wonder came in to meet Berry Gordy and play the piano. He jokingly tells me how he and his friends, fellow band members said, "who is this little blind boy; I wonder what this little blind boy is going to do?" He told me when Stevie Wonder sat down to play the piano, they all fell silent and their laughter moved to sheer amazement. I laughed so hard when he shared this story with me. He also played with Sammy Davis Jr. at the annual NAACP event which was his favorite event.

Out of all the stories my dad has recanted there two that really stand out for me. The first is his march with Dr. Martin Luther King, Jr. in Detroit as a band member playing his trumpet behind supportive marchers. Wow! I'm reliving history in the moment of hearing this story. The second historical gem shared by my dad is that he was one of the first African American musicians to play in the Detroit Symphony Orchestra. He says to me in a very matter of fact tone of voice, "I was a fill-in for when other musicians couldn't make it or had emergency situations. I didn't really like this 'gig,' my preference was to play in a jazz band or with Motown." I did a little digging and found out these things happened before I was even born. In these moments I find myself smack dab in the middle of history, heritage, and legacy...What a blessing.

The daily routine that I remember as a child, was him practicing his trumpet at a certain time after he came home from work. I also remember him on a regular basis putting on his black tuxedo, grabbing his trumpet and heading out of the house. I had no idea that he was living such a wonderful part of Motown and working with such great Legends. He told me about a time when he toured Europe with the Temptations for 30 days. When he returned from that trip, he said, "I'm never going to travel like that again, that's too long to be away from my family." He also shared with me a story about one of the times he traveled with Motown down South with the Temptations. He played several shows where there

was a white line dividing those in the audience - whites on one side and blacks on the other. He remembers vividly exiting the venue to board the bus and being escorted out of town by the police in front of the bus and in back of the bus. I asked him if he was scared, he said, "no, it was just what we did." He would continue to take this same tour with the Temptations for years. My dad also fondly remembers the show when the dividing white line finally came down. "What a day that was," he exclaimed! "It was such a good feeling!"

I tell you talking to my dad is like walking through a history book. My dad continued to work for Motown for years until the time when they finally moved to California. He told me about the phone call he received from Berry Gordy who asked him to come with Motown to California. My dad declined the offer with this response, "LA is no place for me to raise my family." I had no idea that all of this was going on in my childhood, and however, as I look at his responses they are so consistent and so authentic to who he is as a father.

My memories as a child were that my dad was fully present being a father in our lives. Again, as the baby of six, my dad took us to play baseball, ice skating, and he even took my brother and I to *The 20 Grand*, matinée shows. For all of you who are not familiar with the Detroit area, *The 20 Grand* is where all of the Motown legends would perform on a regular basis. It was one of Detroit's most famous night clubs.

I could go on and on about my dad and the beautiful, nostalgic stories he shares with me on our Tuesday / Thursday date nights, which are so dear to me. He is 87 years old and I love learning about his life and all of these special moments. All of the fond memories and the stories shared by my father play into my feelings of being blessed.

HOW DID I MANAGE THIS EMOTION?

I intentionally live in those moments with him. We both share the love of music, so whenever we are together — whether we're going to the movies, to a restaurant, or to visit others — I make sure I have Sammy Davis Jr. playing on the radio in my car. This evokes more nostalgic memories and he loves to hear the trumpets playing in the background of Sammy Davis Jr.'s songs. He smiles, he giggles, and taps his foot to the beat of the music (for you musicians and music lovers, it's that 4/4 time signature beat). I love it and again I feel blessed. In this moment, I recognize in the background it's the very music that I used to hear him practice at home when I was a little girl.

HOW DID I MANAGE THE SOCIAL SETTING?

Not only do I live in this moment, I purposely recreate it every week. It's amazing how he can tell the same story over and over again as if he's telling it for the first time and because the time I spend with him is a blessing, I listen intently to him as if I'm hearing it for the very first time. I try to pick out new elements of the story that I may have missed previously. Or, I will notice his body language and how his face lights up when he talks about working with Sammy Davis, Jr. and Nancy Wilson. I love these moments. They will forever be a part of my memory and a piece of my heart. They truly make me feel so blessed.

IF FACED WITH THIS SITUATION AGAIN, WHAT WOULD I DO DIFFERENTLY:

Not a thing. These moments are special just the way they are and I'm intentional about creating and recreating them every chance I get.

LESSONS LEARNED FROM THIS EMOTION:

Sad things happen in life. Losing my mom was indeed one of the saddest things I've ever experienced, however, I found a blessing in the sadness that has been so special to me and I am truly am grateful for this time with my dad and getting to experience the legacy of who he is and what he will leave behind. Thank you, Daddy.

My experience with this emotion:

How did I manage this emotion?

How did I manage the social setting?

Lessons learned from this emotion:

If faced with this situation again, what would I do differently:

REFLECTIONS

CONFIDENT

Confident –"Having or showing assurance and self-reliance."

- Merriam-Webster's Dictionary

MY EXPERIENCE WITH THIS EMOTION:

Years ago my girlfriend and I would meet at a coffee shop where a quote on the wall said, "when you're confident, you're beautiful."

We chose this coffee shop as "our" coffee shop because of that quote. We would often repeat this quote amid many conversations. I think this backdrop is important as I share my experience with the emotion of feeling confident. Leaving corporate America and starting my own business was truly a leap of faith. I was not confident as a business owner. Every day I would wake with "what ifs." There were so many things I didn't know, but there were a couple of things I knew I was good at —coaching and facilitating.

So I take you back to a meeting with my first big client. I can remember being called into a large health care organization in my home state to coach a group of physicians. As I traveled to this new client the day prior to our meeting, I was filled with a lot of self-talk - some positive, some negative.

I walked into this meeting and there were two department heads and a Vice President sitting at a round table with their notebooks and pens waiting to ask for my advice and write down what I had to say. "What a moment." At this moment, I recognized that I was functioning as a consultant. The conversation in my mind was, "They want to hear what I have to say? What could I tell them? Pay attention, Cathy, you know something! Fake it 'til you make it."

Fast forward years later, I walked into another meeting with a prospective new client, the CEO of the organization, along with two members of her executive team, and I sat waiting at a similar roundtable. Only two of them had notebooks and pens and I was okay with that. As I pulled my seat out from under the table, I noticed that I was not nervous. I was happy to be here in this space. As the meeting began, the CEO explained what she was looking for from my company. As I listened, the emotion of *Confidence* bubbles up and I am solely focused on my client and the needs of this large organization, and self-assured in my ability to provide everything she needs.

HOW DID I MANAGE THIS EMOTION?

I allowed it to have free expression in the moment. It oozed all over my inner soul. It was delightful. I could feel my body language adjusting to the feeling inside. I was sitting a little taller and comfortable in my skin. No need to quiet or engage in negative self-talk or fake it 'til I make it. I'm confident in my abilities to fulfill my roles as coach, consultant and facilitator. Aaah. It feels good. It's all about the client.

HOW DID I MANAGE THE SOCIAL SETTING?

After I listened intently to my client's needs, watching their body language and facial expressions, I asked a few thought-provoking questions that were solely focused on their needs. I noticed the gears turning in their heads and the emotions displayed on their faces. I comfortably sat in the silence to give them an opportunity to express themselves. Internally, I'm at peace because I'm confident. No chatter in my head, I'm listening with my heart.

After leaving this meeting, I remembered a special moment that happened while facilitating a "Leader as Coach" training session. I always ask the class, "What's the difference between arrogance and confidence?" Of course, I always receive varying responses. I've asked this question to hundreds of participants and this is the best response thus far: "Confidence is 'I know what I know.' Arrogance is 'Only I know.'"(An arrogant person thinks they are the only one who knows everything.) I love it! In this moment of reminiscing, I recognized, "I know what I know, and I own it!"

IF FACED WITH THIS SITUATION AGAIN, WHAT WOULD I DO DIFFERENTLY?

Looking back, I would have owned my confidence a lot sooner. Everything is a process, and as I write, I recognize this moment came at an organically perfect time, so I guess I'm right where I'm supposed to be.

LESSONS LEARNED FROM THIS EMOTION?

I go back to the sign I started with at the coffee shop - "When you're confident, you're beautiful." This beauty exudes from the inside out. Confidence to me means I've put in the work externally to hone my craft and am committed to continual growth and development personally and professionally. I now realize in this moment of confidence, I'm feeling so good on the inside that I can focus solely on others. I love being in this space. Yessssss! "When you're confident, you're beautiful."

My experience with this emotion:

____

____

____

____

____

How did I manage this emotion?

____

____

____

____

____

How did I manage the social setting?

____

____

____

____

____

Lessons learned from this emotion:

____

____

____

____

____

If faced with this situation again, what would I do differently:

____

____

____

____

____

REFLECTIONS

CONNECTED

Connected –"Bring together or into contact so that a real link is established."

- Oxford Dictionary

MY EXPERIENCE WITH THIS EMOTION:

It's been 52 months since my mom's death. I sometimes use months to describe the time frame…it seems to make it more bearable to accept. It was a Friday afternoon, and I was hanging curtains. Something I had not done since my kids were toddlers and they are now well into their 30s. I took the curtains out of the package and realized I had to iron them. I ran upstairs to the laundry room and threw the curtains on the ironing board and all of a sudden a childhood memory came rushing in reminding me of my mom used to iron curtains. It was vivid like it just happened a month ago. The memory suddenly evoked an army of emotions. A smile of gratitude - so thankful to have the memory – moved to pain in my heart because of the void. Heartbreak suddenly shifted to great pride. I never considered myself a traditional "housewife," however, my mom was. She made curtains, presented home cooked meals, planted flowers…all of the things that fall under the job description of "Housewife." I never considered myself to be that and I could never fill her shoes in that way. In this moment of

ironing curtains – I felt a strong connection to her. It brought me great joy to be in this space and recognize that so many things I watched her do, I am now doing.

Ahhhh, what a strong sense of connectedness to my mom. I cherish this link to just a small part of the legacy she left behind. In this very minute, my grief shifted to a place where I can think of her, smile and be grateful for the memories. It's been four years and four months since I've seen or talked to my mom, and I'm okay. I'm living the legacy she left behind…Now that's a connection.

HOW DID I MANAGE THIS EMOTION?

I allowed the emotion to have its full expression, which led to a plethora of emotions bubbling up. Isn't that just like a real conversation? You start off talking about one topic and several other subjects rise up? I find that when I'm courageous enough to just be quiet and listen, the dominant emotion speaks the loudest. Connected is the emotion dominating this internal conversation.

HOW DID I MANAGE THE SOCIAL SETTING?

There's no one here in this moment but me and the precious memories of my mom. I allowed this emotion to have its full expression. When my mom first passed away, I intentionally sought out older women to fill the void. There are two older women that I refer to as my "spiritual moms," and I have felt a strong connection to their heart and soul. They have been a blessing in my life.

LESSONS LEARNED FROM THIS EMOTION?

There are many things I have avoided since my mom passed, wearing her necklace, because I don't want her scent to fade away because I can't "take it" that she's not here listening to a voicemail from her that I saved, having pictures of her on display in my office or home because I only want to look at her when I'm emotionally ready. Well, this emotion of being connected to her came out of nowhere, unexpected and uninvited. I survived, and found great joy in the pain. My lesson from this emotion is "I will survive."

IF I HAD TO DO IT ALL OVER AGAIN, WHAT WOULD I DO DIFFERENTLY?

Not a thing. I will stay on this emotional roller coaster and ride it 'til the end. It was a pleasant experience and I definitely cherish these memories.

My experience with this emotion:

How did I manage this emotion?

How did I manage the social setting?

Lessons learned from this emotion:

If faced with this situation again, what would I do differently:

REFLECTIONS

COURAGE

Courage –"Mental or moral strength to venture, persevere, and withstand danger, fear or difficulty."

- Merriam-Webster's Dictionary

MY EXPERIENCE WITH THIS EMOTION:

Last year I accepted an assignment to go into an auto parts manufacturer where I planned to facilitate Diversity and Inclusion training. This training would be for 800 employees with the goal of helping this organization create a more inclusive workplace. I have trained several thousand people on diversity and inclusion so I knew I could do it and was up for the challenge. I felt I was good to go so and signed the contract.

Shortly after signing the contract, I discovered that the reason this company requested the training was because someone had hung a noose in the plant. My first thought was, "Really, it's 2018!" After this thought, the emotion of anger emerged. My second thought was, "Would I be safe as a black woman going into this environment teaching this content?" The next emotion that was more dominant was fear. I immediately began to pray about this training. Did I mention it was not in my home state? I was flying across the country for this training. After prayer and asking for wisdom, I was okay with accepting this assignment. This is when I began to feel the emotion of Courage.

At this point, I began to think about how I could ensure that this training would have an impact on 800 people in this environment? I decided to use two really cool elements to enhance the training. I used a snippet from The Temptations movie when they were performing in the South. There was a rope between the audience dividing the whites and the blacks. While this separation happened over 50 years ago, can we still see the physical ropes today? But what about mentally? Are the ropes still in our minds and hearts, and do they show up on a regular basis based on the work environment we create and how we treat one another?

Another element I added to this training was something called the privilege walk. I invite a group of participants to the front of the room and ask a series of questions based on socioeconomic events that they had no control over in their life. Based on their responses to the questions, they would either take one step forward or one step backward. I facilitated this activity seven times with a total of 140 participants who volunteered to engage in this exercise. It was difficult to watch and have the same racial/ethnic group end up in the back of the walk every time.   It was very emotional, thought-provoking and eye-opening for so many. What made this so amazing is I only had an hour to teach each session and manage a room filled with a wide range of emotions to make this training effective. Can you see why I would need courage to navigate this environment? During one of the sessions, I had a heckler shout out and make jokes that were inappropriate, and of course, every heckler has his posse. This was no different. As he stood up, with the stature of Goliath and myself feeling like David, I said a silent prayer. What came out of my mouth next was appropriately challenging to the heckler and seemed to let him know that I meant business. He sat down and I did not hear another peep out of him for the rest of the training.

HOW DID I MANAGE THIS EMOTION?

I allowed the emotion of courage to ooze all through my body. I felt an internal strength that changed my body language and heightened my performance. I walked taller and with even more confidence. I wanted this emotion to linger as long as it could. I allowed it to have its full expression.

HOW DID I MANAGE THE SOCIAL SETTING?

So I know you're dying to hear what I said to the heckler. Well, here it is: "I don't have a noose hanging in my work environment. I didn't come here for jokes or inappropriate conversation or comments. I came here to help YOU. When I leave, I go back to my life with no nooses in my environment, so I hope you will take this opportunity the company is providing to learn how you all can create a better work environment for yourselves. This training is not for me, this is for you." At that moment I felt courageous!

IF FACED WITH THIS SITUATION AGAIN, WHAT WOULD I DO DIFFERENTLY:

Not a thing. I think back to this moment whenever I feel nervous about a training course that I'm getting ready to facilitate and I say to myself, "Remember Goliath the heckler? You got this girl! You can do it!"

LESSONS LEARNED FROM THIS EMOTION:

Fear and intimidation are usually the precursors to courage. I read this quote and it resonated with me, "Without fear, there cannot be courage. (Christopher Paolini) and from this I've created my mantra, "there is no courage without my Heavenly Father." The lesson for me is to continue to be prayerful in moments of fear.

QUESTIONS FROM THE "PRIVILEGE WALK"

NOTE: This is a very "high risk" activity that requires trust building and safety for participants; introducing this activity too early in the training or before building trust risks creating resentment and hurt that can inhibit further sharing and openness.

PRIVILEGE WALK STATEMENTS

- If you are a white male take one step forward.
- If there have been times in your life when you skipped a meal because there was no food in the house take one step backward.
- If you have visible or invisible disabilities take one step backward.
- If you attended (grade) school with people you felt were like yourself take one step forward.
- If you grew up in an urban setting take one step backward.
- If your family had health insurance take one step forward.
- If your work holidays coincide with religious holidays that you celebrate take one step forward.

- If you feel good about how your identified culture is portrayed by the media take one step forward.
- If you have been the victim of physical violence based on your gender, ethnicity, age or sexual orientation take one step backward.
- If you have ever felt passed over for an employment position based on your gender, ethnicity, age or sexual orientation take one step backward.
- If you were born in the United States take one step forward.
- If English is your first language take one step forward.
- If you have been divorced or impacted by divorce take one step backward.
- If you came from a supportive family environment take one step forward.
- If you have completed high school take one step forward.
- If you were able to complete college take one step forward.
- If you are a citizen of the United States take one step forward.
- If you took out loans for your education take one step backward.
- If you attended private school take one step forward.
- If you have ever felt unsafe walking alone at night take one step backward.

*Credit - This activity was adapted for Lake Land College by the Diversity Education Task Force.

My experience with this emotion:

How did I manage this emotion?

How did I manage the social setting?

Lessons learned from this emotion:

If faced with this situation again, what would I do differently:

REFLECTIONS

REFLECTIONS

DEFEATED

Defeated –"Having been beaten in a battle or other contest."

- Merriam-Webster's Dictionary

MY EXPERIENCE WITH THIS EMOTION:

About two years after my mom passed, I was deep into this emotion. Not because of my own grief, (as if that wasn't bad enough) but because of my empathic nature, I could physically and emotionally feel my dad's grief. It was and still is very painful. However, I only recently discovered the immense value of this emotion. Before recognizing and sitting with this it, I was always caught up in the loop of trying to "fix it" for my dad; always trying to make him feel better. While in the moment, there might have been some brief snippets of relief for him...For example, a slight smile, or a moment of wonder as he glances at my grandchildren. My dad loves children, especially babies...he refers to them as a miracle. But once that moment was over, I could still feel and see his grief. Every day I would try to "fix it" no matter what! This intense desire and need to make his grief all better just would not go away.

Four years later, it's still there, just less intense. As well it should be! My mom and dad were married for 64 years. They were childhood sweethearts, so they were together for 70 years. From their relationships sprang six children, 21 grandchildren, and 18 great-grandchildren. Why did I think I could ever "fix that?!!!"

It wasn't until I "listened" to my own emotion of defeat that I was finally able to support my dad in a different way. This emotion sometimes felt like a heavy boulder sitting on my chest with a great heaviness of heart, and no matter how hard I tried to lift it, I just couldn't. I consider myself to be pretty strong, but this boulder was just too heavy for me as my battle or contest was definitely an internal struggle. It was in the emotion of defeat that helped me to stop trying to "fix it"/lift the boulder. In this moment, I asked myself, "What would happen if instead of trying to move this boulder, what if I just sat on top of it? What would happen if I asked my dad to join me?"

HOW DID I MANAGE THIS EMOTION?

By allowing myself to sit with this emotion and allowing it to have its full expression. I received the message from this quiet space of "Stop trying to take away his pain Cathy, It's not easy fix."

HOW DID I MANAGE THE SOCIAL SETTING?

Now when my dad says, "I sure do miss my wife." Instead of talking about a time when he will see her again, (trying to fix it) I ask him, "What do you miss most about her?" In some respects, I invite him to sit on the boulder with me. I intentionally ask questions that will open his heart such as, "What do you want her to know that you didn't get a chance to tell her?" "What do you miss most about her?" The responses I get to these questions bring about a secure environment with a free-flowing fluid conversation that allows room for an array of emotions. I/we absolutely love!!!

LESSONS LEARNED FROM THIS EMOTION:

By allowing defeat to have its full expression within me internally, I was now able to let my dad have space to fully express his grief without trying to fix it. "Love your neighbor as you love yourself." I can't do for others what I had not done for myself.

IF FACED WITH THIS SITUATION AGAIN, WHAT WOULD I DO DIFFERENTLY

Shh...Just Listen, Cathy. I would have sat in the silence sooner so that I could hear what this emotion was trying to tell me. "Great things happen in the silence."

My experience with this emotion:

How did I manage this emotion?

How did I manage the social setting?

Lessons learned from this emotion:

If faced with this situation again, what would I do differently:

REFLECTIONS

REFLECTIONS

DEPRESSED

Depressed–"Being perplexed or disconcerted."

- Merriam-Webster's Dictionary

MY EXPERIENCE WITH THIS EMOTION:

My time spent with this emotion was very difficult. I was in the valley of depression some 20 years ago. This emotion did not come and go or rise and fall, like the rest. It took up residence within me and lingered for quite some time. Initially, I could not articulate how I was feeling. I knew I felt weak physically, mentally and emotionally. I felt empty! In my late 20's early 30's I thought I was superwoman, always flying around trying to rescue someone. However, during this time all of the busyness in my life came to a screeching halt. In my weakened state, I no longer had the energy to put on my cape and fly off to save others. I was keenly aware that I needed to focus on myself and figure out who would rescue me.

I can remember the internal darkness and the emptiness that enveloped my soul and spirit. I immediately wanted to go back to what was comfortable for me which was being a mom. So, I quit my full-time job and went back home to take care of my family.

The thought of sending my three children off to school with a hot breakfast and a nicely packed lunch every day brought a flicker of light to my soul. However, that flicker was quickly extinguished the following Monday when my children who were 11, 13, 15 at the time awakened early, made their own breakfast and lunch and headed off to school before I got out of bed. I was devastated and felt like my children didn't need me anymore. I then had a bright idea…I asked my husband if we could have another baby, he quickly said, "NOOOOOO!" One of the best decisions he ever made, however, I didn't think so at the time. For this decision meant that I could not go back to taking care of someone who was completely dependent upon me…a new baby.

His decline to my request moved me to think about other relationships in my life. I began to ask myself, "Are most of the relationships in my life dependent upon me being the caregiver?" Spending time with this question felt like being punched in the stomach. I found it painfully perplexing to ponder this question. However, I knew I had to.

HOW DID I MANAGE THIS EMOTION?

So here I sit face to face with this villain called Depression. What is it? I discovered it to be many things, but one definition is, anger turned inward over an extended period of time (a repressed, emotion without a voice and no one to listen). So I asked myself, "What are you angry about?" I was angry because I couldn't answer the more important question, "Who am I?"

I was afraid to deal with this anger and emptiness alone. I didn't know what I liked to do, what my favorite foods were or what filled me up. What were the things that nurtured my heart, mind and soul? I didn't know. I felt as if I had so many emotions unheard and repressed, I found myself in a deep dark valley feeling so low and depressed. I knew I would need help from others to climb out of this darkness. I had a team that seemed to have lowered a rope to help me climb out of this hole. That would include my Heavenly Father, friends, family, and a psychotherapist. (Yes, therapy. For some reason this seems to be a kept secret in the African American culture). However, I found therapy very helpful and it proved to be a specific time in the week where I could solely focus on me.

Finally, without looking for distractions or blaming others, I did a lot of soul searching and began seeking wisdom, as I daily pondered the question, "Who Am I?" However, my therapy sessions were only once a week and I felt like I needed to talk about what I was experiencing on a daily basis. During therapy, I was introduced to the beautiful gift of journaling. It would prove to be a place where I could explore and give voice to a cadre of emotions that bubbled up on a regular basis. I truly begin to fill my empty reservoir on a regular basis. I discovered that I love Bible reading, prayer, journaling, meditation, and exercising, and I made a vow to myself that I would no longer live a life without listening to my internal voice.

HOW DID I MANAGE THE SOCIAL SETTING?

I seemed to be quite comfortable taking care of others. For most of my friendships seemed to be one-sided. When I tried to change the dynamics of some of those relationships and look for support, most of them would not budge. They seem to want things to stay the same. Some would even say, "No, you don't look depressed. You can't be depressed, you're our rock." This lead to additional frustration and anger. I realized that I would not receive in return what I had given out, so from this point, I began to have crucial conversations, that would set boundaries and expectations on what I was looking for in relationships. I came to appreciate that healthy relationships are reciprocal, so I began to change the dynamics of my current relationships and I sought out new friends. I now find myself in healthy relationships that are indeed reciprocal and rewarding. Having those conversations was not always easy, but they proved to be valuable in yielding the results I was seeking. In my personal life, I have a group of friends that are an absolute joy to be around. It is in these social settings that I now find great joy and satisfaction.

IF FACED WITH THIS SITUATION AGAIN, WHAT WOULD I DO DIFFERENTLY:

I married young and had children right away, so I feel like I really didn't have an opportunity to ask or answer the question, "Who am I?" For years, I patterned myself after my mom, I watched her and mimicked what I saw. This made me happy for a while, but when that no longer worked, I needed to establish my own identity. One piece of advice I always give new moms is, "don't lose who you are as you step into this new role as a mom." It's so easy to do. As moms, we're happy to take car of this new bundle of joy along with everyone else. However, I've learned when I could answer the question, "Who am I? I was able to set appropriate boundaries that would allow me to give myself permission to listen and respond to the needs of what is going on inside of me.

LESSONS LEARNED FROM THIS EMOTION:

All the years I spent running around taking care of other people, I was not focusing on my needs. Since I'm being honest, I was such a caregiver that I didn't even know I had needs. As women, we go through so many changes, and function in so many different roles that we either sacrifice ourselves too much or forget about what we need. Once, we're too tired to care for others, we might try to do something for ourselves and then we experience the emotion of guilt and because that doesn't feel as good as care-taking, we go back to caring for others. It's a vicious cycle. The biggest lesson for me was to learn to value myself enough to listen to my voice as it cried out for attention. With all of the attention I was giving other people, my internal voice would say, "Who's going to take care of me?" Once I was able to answer the question, Who am I? I could then begin to listen to the voice inside of me. Finding my identity allowed me to take care of myself in a way that was very meaningful to me. Knowing who you are also means knowing what you like and understanding what fills your bucket and nurtures your soul. Once I found those things then I gave myself permission to engage in guilt-free self-care. This was no easy journey, but so worth all of the effort. It's been 20 years and I haven't found myself back in the valley again, so I guess the lesson I finally learned is, "Love your neighbor as you love YOURSELF!"

My experience with this emotion:

How did I manage this emotion?

How did I manage the social setting?

Lessons learned from this emotion:

If faced with this situation again, what would I do differently:

REFLECTIONS

REFLECTIONS

ECSTASY

Ecstasy–"A state of overwhelming emotion; rapturous delight."

- Merriam-Webster's Dictionary

MY EXPERIENCE WITH THIS EMOTION:

I often ask myself why this emotion seems to have been limited to the bedroom? I'd like to share a moment of Ecstasy that was so beautiful I will never forget it. About five years ago, I started taking singing lessons. I was one of those people who "couldn't carry a tune in a bucket." However, my son has this amazing voice and for years, I have proclaimed he got it from me. Everyone in my family would chime in and say, "Nooooo, we don't think so!" I've always wanted to stand in front of a group and sing - not just sing, but sound good.

So back to these singing lessons. I was at my first vocal lesson and my instructor says, "okay, sing a song for me." I start out singing Gladys Knight's "Midnight Train to Georgia." After about two minutes in he stops me and says, "Okay, you have great stage presence, but we have to make that voice match that stage presence." I laughed, but deep down inside I felt like my family must have been right all of these years. This was my introduction to my vocal coach's strong personality who would not and did

not sugar coat any of his feedback or coaching. I would be in this relationship for years.

When you're taking singing lessons, there is a whole process of getting comfortable with your voice. Think about what it's like to speak into the microphone...when you hear yourself and step away from the microphone, most say internally, "I hate the way my voice sounds." Now imagine having that feeling every week for 30 minutes, but instead of telling yourself you don't like your voice, your instructor says, "No that's not right, we need to change that!"

This process of getting comfortable with my voice took months of practice. After time, not only was I comfortable with my voice, I began to like my voice.

I will never forget the singing lesson I had when I fell in love with my voice. It was a Wednesday night around 8:15 pm and the song I'd been practicing for months was Whitney Houston's "I Believe In You and Me."I started singing in head voice, then fluctuated to chest voice, into vibrato, and held my note for at least 20 seconds. I could not believe this was me!

HOW DID I MANAGE THIS EMOTION?

It was so beautiful that I remember it as I write, but it had to be managed. I wanted to jump for joy literally, but I harnessed this moment of ecstasy until the end of the song. It was a glorious energy that moved through my body. As I listened to my voice, I for the first time felt like a human instrument. Not just my voice - because it takes the entire body to create the beauty of vocal harmony - but my entire body was feeling ecstasy because at this moment I fell in love with my voice.

HOW DID I MANAGE THE SOCIAL SETTING?

As I was singing this song, I was also waiting for my instructor to stop me. When I would sing notes that were wrong, he would stop me and say, "Oh no, back up, do it this way!" I'm now more than halfway through the song and he was smiling and nodding his head. I really am managing a lot of emotions in this moment.

Remember, my instructor held no punches and was stingy with praise. I saw for the first time pride, approval, and joy on his face. Can you imagine the energy in the room?? I still needed to manage all of this because I wanted to finish this song. I focused on the end result. I also thought about Whitney Houston and how flawlessly she sang and tried to imitate her.

IF FACED WITH THIS SITUATION AGAIN, WHAT WOULD I DO DIFFERENTLY:

Nothing. This moment is perfect. It's ecstasy!

LESSONS LEARNED FROM THIS EMOTION:

Honestly, I was shocked that I could feel this emotion outside of the bedroom. I know for sure there are other things in life that evoke sheer ecstasy and I have discovered a few more in addition to singing; sitting in nature and noticing the personality of my creator is rapturously delightful. I find things that involve my entire being - my heart, soul, mind, and spirit is what evokes ecstasy for me. I'm ever on the lookout for this emotion. Especially since it's no longer confined to the bedroom.

My experience with this emotion:

How did I manage this emotion?

How did I manage the social setting?

Lessons learned from this emotion:

If faced with this situation again, what would I do differently:

REFLECTIONS

EXCITED

Excited–"Having, showing, or characterized by a heightened state of energy, enthusiasm, eagerness, etc."

- Merriam-Webster's Dictionary

MY EXPERIENCE WITH THIS EMOTION:

Recently, I had an opportunity to reconnect with my childhood best friend. We lived on the same street until I was 13 and she was 12. Our friendship continued after I moved away. She was my maid of honor at my wedding. Circumstances changed and eventually, we lost contact. So here we are 40+ years later back together again. There are many reasons for my joy and enthusiasm, but I will share just a few.

I'm amazed at how our conversation picked up where we left off as if no time has passed. We, of course, fill in the blanks of the many years apart, but the ease and flow of our conversation was so beautiful. It touches my heart and soul. One thing about Tracey and me is we love to laugh. Reminiscing about our days as kids and teenagers warms my soul and spirit.

She has taken me back to cooking hamburgers in my Easy-Bake Oven for our community restaurant to making mud pies in the backyard. We also reminisce about playing at Peterson Park most of the day until we hear the street lights begin to ignite, then we would run home at full speed to beat our curfew. That time changed based on when darkness fell. It would be 9:00 pm in the summertime, and 6:00 pm in the winter. And yes, we played outside in the wintertime. Ice skating, building snowmen, and snowball fights. Those were such good times!

However, this isn't the best part about this reunion. The absolute best part is that she can say my name just like my mom used to say it! And I love hearing it! She reminded me of a lot of childhood memories that we shared. This walk down memory lane was so exciting. We have committed to regular lunch dates and face time phone calls. I love having her in my life. There's something about a friend that has known you since childhood and I'm so grateful to have her in my life.

HOW DID I MANAGE THIS EMOTION?

Emotions rise and fall, come and go. Writing about the emotion of being excited has evoked another emotion which is Gratitude! I also sit with this emotion and smile from the inside out.

HOW DID I MANAGE THE SOCIAL SETTING?

We were reunited at a bridal shower. We hugged, laughed and cried together on this particular day. We exchanged numbers and promised to connect. I knew I wanted this kind of energy and nostalgia in my life. So I reached out within two weeks to have lunch. Every time we're together, I let her know how much I love and appreciate her. Yes, I'm still excited about this relationship.

LESSONS LEARNED FROM THIS EMOTION:

I'm grateful to have spent my childhood growing up with Tracey and I'm excited about our future together now that we're both in our fifties. I read an article that said, "Good friends cannot be determined by the amount of time you've spent apart: If when you finally reunite and your conversations feel as if no time has passed, more than likely you have a solid friendship."

My lesson learned has been the truthfulness of this statement. We acknowledge that time has passed, but we are catching up with joy, laughter, and much appreciation for each other. Ahhhh yes… gratitude.

IF FACED WITH THIS SITUATION AGAIN, WHAT WOULD I DO DIFFERENTLY:

Of course, I would like to say I would put forth an effort to reconnect sooner, however, I think this reunion came at just the right time. Any sooner, and I may not have had the time or the level of appreciation I have now.

My experience with this emotion:

How did I manage this emotion?

How did I manage the social setting?

Lessons learned from this emotion:

If faced with this situation again, what would I do differently:

REFLECTIONS

REFLECTIONS

FEAR

Fear–"An unpleasant often strong emotion caused by anticipation or awareness of danger; anxious concern."

- Merriam-Webster's Dictionary

MY EXPERIENCE WITH THIS EMOTION:

Out of all of the emotions I've experienced, this one is the loudest. It screams, yells, and refuses to be ignored. It has a mind of its own and it can hold me captive if I allow it. Oh yes, I've experienced it many times, leaving corporate America to start my own business, recording my first TV show, being interviewed by Doug Llewelyn, becoming a mom, and the list goes on....

The most recent is...writing this book. So many fears. Fear of it not being good enough. I'm pretty open and vulnerable in this book, so the fear of being judged. Fear of failure. Fear of success. Yes, I'm anxious about a lot of things surrounding this book. There have been so many times where I just wanted to give up. However, once the fear was less intense, I felt compelled to continue to write for so many reasons. I have coached hundreds and trained thousands and I've seen firsthand what it's like when the struggle to articulate our emotions leaves us feeling confused, frustrated, and sometimes angry. I pride myself on creating a safe space for my clients to discover, explore, and come face to face with their fear. Now, how would I respond with it staring me right in the face?

HOW DID I MANAGE THIS EMOTION?

Self-talk. All the coaching questions I would ask a client, I asked myself. I also have an executive coach, and I've been coached on this at least three times. I follow the steps of emotional intelligence and I intentionally validate this unpleasantly strong emotion. I say to myself, "You have every right to feel this way Cathy, this is a valid emotion around this project." The big question was, would I allow it to rise and fall, come and go like most emotions, or would I consistently feed this emotion so that it would grow and become strong enough to control me? To hold me down and keep me captive?

Years ago, I read the book, *"Feel the Fear and Do It Anyway,"* so to continue applying the lessons I learned from this book, I have adopted this as my mantra. 'Feel the fear and do it anyway.' Even writing about it right now is so cathartic. It still pays me a visit on a regular basis and I remind myself that I can't control the emotions that bubble up, but I can control how I respond to them. I also noticed, as soon as this emotion dissipates, there is this passionate desire that burns from my belly that is more vibrant and combustible than the emotion of fear that fuels me to move forward and create a space for others to manage their emotions. Shh..Just Listen.

HOW DID I MANAGE THE SOCIAL SETTING?

Often this emotion is between me, myself, and I. Until I shared it with my coach, friends, and family. Friends and family tend to want to fix it. (Don't we all want to fix it?). I'm sure once this book is published, I will experience a new kind of fear – may be even more intense. At that moment, I will grab this book and function as the reader and not the author and will journal on the subsequent pages.

LESSONS LEARNED FROM THIS EMOTION:

I think Marianne Williamson says it best. I've heard and read this poem many times before but never has it resonated so deeply with me than at this time in my life in relation to this book. I've learned and have felt the truthfulness of the poem, *"Our Deepest Fear"*—

> *Our deepest fear is not that we are inadequate. Our deepest fear is that we are powerful beyond measure. It is our light, not our darkness that most frightens us. We ask ourselves, Who am I to be brilliant, gorgeous, talented, and fabulous? Actually, who are you not to be? You are a child of God. Your playing small does not serve the world. There is nothing enlightened about shrinking so that other people will not feel insecure around you. We are all meant to shine, as children do. We were born to make manifest the glory of God that is within us. It is not just in some of us; it is in everyone and as we let our own light shine, we unconsciously give others permission to do the same. As we are liberated from our own fear, our presence automatically liberates others.*

IF FACED WITH THIS SITUATION AGAIN, WHAT WOULD I DO DIFFERENTLY:

I would not have allowed this emotion to hold me captive for so long. I have noticed along the journey of writing this book, that once I really managed my fear, I could tap deeper into my heart and soul while recanting my stories. They became more vivid in my mind and begin to flow smoothly from my heart. For this reason alone, I would have worked harder to manage it sooner. (See if you can tell which stories were written before I was able to manage my fear and those that were written after.) Shh..Just Listen.

My experience with this emotion:

How did I manage this emotion?

How did I manage the social setting?

Lessons learned from this emotion:

If faced with this situation again, what would I do differently:

REFLECTIONS

GIFTED

Gifted – "Having a great natural ability."

- Merriam-Webster's Dictionary

MY EXPERIENCE WITH THIS EMOTION:

I'm sitting on my patio as the sun began to set. I've started this thing of watching outdoor concerts on YouTube. My selection tonight is Kirk Whalum with George Duke playing Celine Dion's *"Because You Love Me."* The music is beautiful indeed! But what is more beautiful to me is how Kirk Whalum consistently creates a space for other artists to stand in their greatness.

In this video, everything about Kirk Whalum's body language says, "You're pretty amazing, George. I'm going to enjoy your God-given talent, and your gift. This time, space and moment is all about you." Kirk Whalum humbly steps into the background to let George Duke perform the most beautiful rendition of the Celine Dion's song that I've ever heard. I'm truly amazed at his natural ability to make the piano sing this song. He is indeed gifted and I'm feeling that way at this moment as well. (Note - Link to Youtube video - https://youtu.be/hNICl8RuxLI)

HOW DID I MANAGE THIS EMOTION?

This emotion resonates with me so deeply because as a Leadership Coach, I often stand in the background and happily create a space for my clients to discover their natural abilities (God-given talents) and step into their greatness. However, during my coaching sessions, I'm always living in the moment, I'm never able to stand outside the coaching session to see what it actually looks like. Well, while watching this YouTube video, I saw it in action with Kirk Whalum and it was so beautiful. What a gift to recognize your gift and to operate in that space. It truly is mind, body, soul and spirit. In this moment, I truly feel gifted.

HOW DID I MANAGE THE SOCIAL SETTING:

While fully enjoying this emotion and allowing it to have its full expression, I move to a place of deep gratitude that I have found my gift and I'm able to use it every day to make people feel special, empowered, confident, loved, supported and vibrant. (I could go on and on with a list of emotions.) I grabbed my journal and began to capture this moment. I spent time with myself externally (this video allowed me to have a moment where I felt like I was outside of myself looking in on a coaching session.) In this space, my heart, soul, and mind feel nurtured. What a gift! I bowed my head and offered a prayer of appreciation and gratitude.

LESSONS LEARNED FROM THIS EMOTION:

There was a time in my life when I didn't know what my natural gifts and talents were, so I could not intentionally use them. I knew that I would always bring a certain energy to any room and that people were always very comfortable telling me their deepest thoughts, feelings, and emotions. My gift is that I'm a very empathic person. I can actually feel what other people feel. I've heard empathy defined as, "put your heart into the heart of the listener." I'm able to do that with ease. For years I didn't know that and definitely could not articulate it. It wasn't until I went to school for coaching that I discovered there was a name for my gift. Empathic! Once, I discovered it, I began to put it to use intentionally in personal relationships and professionally as well. With every gift and/or talent the one who possesses has to learn how to use it effectively. So I spent some time learning to do just that. I had to give myself boundaries and create plenty of downtime and self-care to replenish.

Can you imagine walking around being able to feel what other people feel all of the time? It's like when Superman was learning how to use his X-ray vision and his superpowers. I'm sure there were things he saw that he didn't necessarily need to see. Well, in discovering this gift, there were things I could feel in others that I didn't always want or need to feel. Then, there was the whole process of learning how to separate the feelings of others from my own feelings. It is a gift, but I had to learn how and when to use it. So with all of that being said, the lesson I learned is that our natural (God-given) gifts and talents are beautiful when used appropriately in service to others and ultimately bring glory to the giver, my Heavenly Father...Yes...I feel gifted!!!

IF FACED WITH THIS SITUATION AGAIN, WHAT WOULD I DO DIFFERENTLY:

NOTHING. This moment is perfect.

My experience with this emotion:

How did I manage this emotion?

How did I manage the social setting?

Lessons learned from this emotion:

If faced with this situation again, what would I do differently:

REFLECTIONS

REFLECTIONS

GRATITUDE

Gratitude –"The state of being grateful."

- Merriam-Webster's Dictionary

MY EXPERIENCE WITH THIS EMOTION:

My experience with this emotion comes frequently when I think back to my childhood. I'm the baby of six children and growing up in a large family was so much fun. I will share just a few things that take me to a place of gratitude, puts a smile on my face and warms my heart. I also want you to remember as I share these things that I'm sharing them from the perspective of an African American family living in the early 1960s, 70s and 80s.

Growing up, we were always the first black family on the street. At the time I didn't really recognize what that meant, but I do now - some would probably say "privileged." My parents really enjoyed life and always made sure that we studied hard and got good grades, and because of that, we played hard. As I look back and reflect, I know my life was balanced, because we always had to take care of the important things first. Like cleaning the house every Saturday afternoon to the sound of Motown tunes. We also

My dad is Eddie Jones, last row, far left. 1967 Michigan State Fair

had to make sure we took care of our spiritual routine. I even appreciated those things because they gave me a sense of security and structure, but after we took care of those things, the fun would begin!

Let's start with summer vacations. We grew up going on vacation for the entire month of August. We would frequently drive across the country and visit some of my dad's musician friends and even stay in some of their homes. The one I remember most vividly was Hamilton Bohannon. This was such an amazing experience. His house was actually built into a mountain and was surrounded by nature, which I loved even back then as a child. I remember his home was full of so many pretty, shiny things. It was such a beautiful experience. The following year we would drive across the country again to Florida and then catch a plane and fly to the Bahamas. During this time, I just thought this was the way things were and everyone must be taking these kinds of vacations. I didn't recognize it was a big deal until my husband and I planned to take our three children to Disney World for a week. We had to scrimp and save and cut back for quite a while in order to pay for this trip. That was the first time I wondered, "How did my parents afford to vacation for a month!?" I'm in a place of gratitude.

Even when we were home, we had glorious weekends where my dad would take my brother and I ice skating and he would skate with us and teach us. I remember those days fondly. In addition to that, we never missed a year of going to the Ice Capades or the Ringling Brothers and Barnum & Bailey Circus.

In the warmer months of the year, we would attend my dad's concerts at Pine Knob with the Temptations, Diana Ross and The Supremes, Four Tops, and the list goes on. My mom would always pack a cooler full of food — it was good times indeed! Remember, my mom is an awesome cook! I'm talking packed in this cooler is fried chicken, homemade potato salad, fried green tomatoes... the works! For those of you not from Michigan, Pine Knob is a venue where they actually have ski slopes and large hills. After my brother and I ate, we climbed those slopes and ran down full speed, screaming and laughing. Good times indeed! Gratitude.

I'm also grateful for the dinner around the kitchen table every day that was a regular daily routine. Imagine eight people sitting around the kitchen table having dinner. In my family, we all have a sense of humor and a quick wit, so dinnertime was so much fun. I recognize as I'm writing that this again gave me structure and security.

I'm also grateful for the large basement we had in our home where all of my siblings convene after dinner. In this space, the six of us watch TV, shoot pool, and then put on our favorite talent shows. We even had Motown costumes where we would get dressed up and perform. I think this talent show was one of the activities that helped to build our confidence because we would perform in front of each other and laugh and talk about each other's performance. And it didn't matter, we would continue our performance and laugh with each other and at each other. Happy times. Gratitude.

HOW DID I MANAGE THIS EMOTION?

I don't think this emotion needs to be managed. I allow it to have its full expression. This emotion starts in my chest and oozes all over my body like a water sprinkler. It truly is a bucket filler.

HOW DID I MANAGE THE SOCIAL SETTING?

I would say in my late 20s when my children were young, I began to feel the weight of parenting and providing for a family. I would often ask myself, "I only have half the children my parents had, how did they do all that they did with six children!?"

Every time I asked that question, I called my mom and told her how much I appreciated them both and how they provided for us. More recently in my 50s, I have become a gratitude junkie - fully believing in and living in the space, but also freely expressing my feelings of gratitude. Being in combat with my mother as we fought and battled cancer for 15 months — oh, there was not a day that went by that I didn't tell my mom how much I appreciated her. She and I spent hours in chemo treatment talking, laughing, and walking down memory lane. These were beautiful moments filled with gratitude. Now, as I spend time with my dad every week and we walk down memory lane together, I frequently express my feelings of gratitude for him. We have the best conversations and there is a warmness in my heart as I write at this moment. I love the emotion of gratitude.

IF FACED WITH THIS SITUATION AGAIN, WHAT WOULD I DO DIFFERENTLY:

Of course, I wish I would have started expressing gratitude towards my parents at a younger age. My husband and I rejoice greatly when we hear our children express their gratitude towards us. So knowing how it feels to receive words of appreciation from your grown children - it's beautiful and a free gift. It's always affordable and it's also the gift that keeps on giving. I wish I would have started this practice much sooner and frequently.

LESSONS LEARNED FROM THIS EMOTION:

Gratitude to me is different than most emotions. For me, it doesn't bubble up from the gut, uninvited. It seems to be triggered by intentional thoughts of appreciation.

Once that thought moves from my head and reaches my chest and is sprinkled all over my heart and soul, then oozes throughout my body, I am impelled/compelled to share my thoughts and feelings of gratitude with the person who evoked this feeling.

I've learned that gratitude has to do with how we think about things. I have the control to visit this space frequently and as much as I'd like. It's a great lesson to remember because my thoughts can change my feelings and out of all the emotions that I've written about, gratitude seems to be one of the most joyous emotions I have felt.

My experience with this emotion:

How did I manage this emotion?

How did I manage the social setting?

Lessons learned from this emotion:

If faced with this situation again, what would I do differently:

REFLECTIONS

REFLECTIONS

GRIEF

Grief – "Deep and poignant distress caused by or as if by bereavement."

- Merriam-Webster's Dictionary

MY EXPERIENCE WITH THIS EMOTION:

For years now, I intentionally have chosen not to know the exact date of my mom's death, however, I can vividly describe when it happened as if it was yesterday. She passed in her sleep. I got the call from my brother, who had received the call from my dad. I drove over to my parents' house to find my dad looking out of the window with a blank stare. I walk in and can't even address his grief. I run to my mom's bed to find her without the breath of life. I love this woman because even in her death she had the look of victory on her face. For she had led a faithful life and even death could not take away her hope of life again.

I've never been this close to death. I've lost people I was close to before, but I had never been this close to the dying process. It's painful, even when you know it's coming. My mom battled lung cancer for 15 months and we anticipated her death for at least three of those months, but nothing can prepare you for the reality. I walk into the room and see my big brother, my only brother (he's 6'7" and had always been a protector in our teenage years) and I see a look on his face I'd never seen on him before, sheer agony. I then glanced down at my father and the pain in my heart was so intense that I can't give it any other name, but GRIEF. It's deeper than hurt, broader than sadness and I was keenly aware that this emotion would be around for a long time. I pulled out my iPad and began to take final pictures of my mom. For I had captured this 15-month journey with pictures, so this was the culmination of what we've fearfully anticipated. I'm grateful I did that.

HOW DID I MANAGE THIS EMOTION?

My next move surprised even me. I then climbed into my mom's bed with her. She still smelled like herself. I'm thankful for this time. I sniffed her intensely because I wanted to be able to recall her smell, even after she was long gone. I laid there for quite some time. I can remember her body hardening (rigor mortis). It didn't matter to me, I still laid there, this was my momma.

In an effort to be considerate, I asked my other siblings if they wanted to climb in her bed and lay with her, and they all said, "Nooooo." It's funny — the thing I feared the most and wanted to stay so far away from — I was now face-to-face with…intimately dancing with death. The cruel enemy that had taken my mom and would leave the emotion of intense grief behind.

HOW DID I MANAGE THE SOCIAL SETTING?

I did not try to take away anyone's pain. I was very aware of my grief. I feel like I intentionally protected myself from things that I would not want to have in my memory. When the coroner came for my mom's body, I went into the basement. I did not want the memory of seeing my mom in a body bag being taken from her home. When my big sister called the funeral home to make arrangements, I moved away from that conversation so that I could not hear it. We really all began to function within the family dynamics. My brother was in my mom's room getting stockings for the outfit she would wear at the funeral. He was going through her underwear drawer. As I write, I think that probably should have been me, but it wasn't because I couldn't and I'm okay with that. I managed this social setting as best I could given the fact I was in a state of shock and grief.

LESSONS LEARNED FROM THIS EMOTION:

That grief will not kill you, it is a process and I intentionally gave myself time and space to grieve. My grief is now intermittent and I do have happy moments in life. Initially, I wondered if I would ever be happy again.

When I was in school for executive coaching one of my instructors, Pat Barlow, said, "You can't experience the height of happiness until you've experienced the depth of sadness." Initially, I questioned this statement, almost didn't believe it until I grieved my mom's death. In losing her, I've experienced the depth of sadness, but my happy moments are richer and happier because I now have a vast chasm in which to make the comparison of intense grief to the height of happiness.

In the words of Destiny's Child - *"I'm a Survivor."* The key for me was not to get stuck in the grief process. I survived and take great solace in the fact that my mom would be so proud of me.

IF FACED WITH THIS SITUATION AGAIN, WHAT WOULD I DO DIFFERENTLY:

Sometimes I think I would have stayed the night and watched her take her last breath, but I don't think I could live with that memory and I don't feel any guilt around not being there, because I was always there. So I will say I don't know if I would do anything differently.

My experience with this emotion:

How did I manage this emotion?

How did I manage the social setting?

Lessons learned from this emotion:

If faced with this situation again, what would I do differently:

REFLECTIONS

GUILT

Guilt –"Feelings of deserving blame especially for imagined offenses or from a sense of inadequacy."

- Merriam-Webster's Dictionary

MY EXPERIENCE WITH THIS EMOTION:

As a leadership coach, I often sit face-to-face with this emotion. I'm able to quickly recognize it when it shows up on some of my clients' faces during a coaching session. However, I do not sit in judgment because I too have frequently visited this space.

In my early 30s I would often experience this emotion in relation to self-care. It seemed as if every time I would set aside an opportunity to do something nice for myself, or just relax, this uninvited guests would knock on the door of my heart and soul. Even though I did not want to answer and let this emotion in, it would break the door down and take up lodging inside of me. This uninvited guest announced itself with a loud internal voice, GUILT! Its entrance came with a lot of questions, "What are you doing relaxing...Isn't that being lazy?" "Why are you just sitting here? There are tons of people you need to help." "What's the purpose of this downtime anyway? It doesn't feel good." I could not stop this voice from talking unless I got up and distracted myself. I did not want to come face-to-face with Guilt.

HOW DID I MANAGE THIS EMOTION?

Back then, I didn't have the knowledge I have now about social and emotional intelligence to manage emotions. So I will start off by saying I did not manage it well. I consistently lived in this space and I didn't understand why I always felt like I had to be moving and/or doing something for someone else??

There were a few times when I tried to sit down to rest and relax, but there was an uneasiness in my belly. The emotion I was feeling was indeed guilt, and because I didn't know how to sit in the silence and listen, I kept running from it. The only time I was able to really relax was when I was completely exhausted and could not move. I truly believe it was my body's way of rescuing me from myself. Yes, I would prove to be the martyr who would save everyone else but not take care of myself. This proved to be a vicious cycle for years.

HOW DID I MANAGE THE SOCIAL SETTING?

Yes, yes, yes, yes and yes! That was my response to every invitation, every favor asked, every request made, yes! I had not empowered myself to say, "No" — no matter how much I longed to. I was not in tune with my emotions or my needs at this point in my life. Not to mention that helping others looks good on the outside, feels good initially (until I'm empty on the inside) and it makes other people happy. This behavior went on for years and I was unable to articulate or figure out what was underneath this quieted and repressed emotion of guilt that turned into anger and resentment. I did not manage social settings well during that time.

IF FACED WITH THIS SITUATION AGAIN, WHAT WOULD I DO DIFFERENTLY:

I would take the time to find out why I was feeling guilty every time I wanted to do something for myself. I've learned as a coach that the emotion of guilt usually rises up when we feel like we have violated our moral compass. Learning how to coach this emotion was very interesting and intriguing to me. So I applied what I learned and took a trip back down memory lane. I indeed discovered that I was running from myself.

So I ask myself the question, "What was the moral compass I felt like I had violated?" I was finally able to figure it out! I thought back to when I was a little girl and how I never saw my mother relax or engage in self-care. My mother had six children and in addition to being a housewife (I mean a real old-fashioned housewife - home cooked meals from scratch, making our clothes, washing and ironing our clothes, cleaning house, making draperies, and the list goes on...), she was also a part-time nurse on the midnight shift. Not to mention, she loved to entertain; she was always planning a party.

Therefore, I did not see my mom taking time out for self-care. As you know from reading other stories, I spent so much of my life mimicking what I saw in her; I grew up to repeat the same behavior. During my journey of finding myself and learning to set boundaries, I began to give myself permission to engage in self-care and to relieve myself from the self-imposed guilt. My mother never said I had to be like her; I just always thought my mom was pretty awesome. However, as a grown woman in my 50s, I am now defining the woman I want to become. During this journey, I shifted from yes, yes, yes, yes to including other responses in my vocabulary such as, "no," or "maybe" and "let me get back with you." I no longer find myself in places where other people expect me to be. I accept invitations based on where I want to be. I've given myself permission to say "no." I finally learned how to manage my time, energy and emotions that allow me to replenish and rejuvenate on a regular basis.

This transformation did not happen overnight - it was a continuous process of sitting with this emotion. I consistently had conversations with myself that sounded a little bit like this — "You deserve this Cathy, you've worked hard." This is like being on an airplane and putting on your oxygen mask before you can assist others…you need to take in oxygen first. I would visually create this image in my head over and over again, and every time I wanted to escape the feelings of guilt, however it was no easy task. Oh, there were feelings of uneasiness. But I sat in the silence, talked myself through it and eventually gave myself permission to find joy in taking care of myself. If I had to do it all over again, I would have mustered up the courage to come face-to-face with the uncomfortable emotion sooner.

LESSONS LEARNED FROM THIS EMOTION:

My whole life I have heard and read these famous words, "Love your neighbor as you love yourself." I didn't truly understand the meaning until I gave myself permission to love me enough to care for myself. When I look back I recognize that without caring for my needs, I was loving my neighbor in spite of myself. Once I was able to manage my guilt and take care of myself properly, my love for others became more genuine, authentic, and rewarding. I began to do things for others out of love for them and my Heavenly Father, instead of out the fear of sitting with myself and running from guilt. What a valuable lesson indeed!

My experience with this emotion:

How did I manage this emotion?

How did I manage the social setting?

Lessons learned from this emotion:

If faced with this situation again, what would I do differently:

REFLECTIONS

HAPPY

Happy –"Enjoying or characterized by well-being and contentment."

- Merriam-Webster's Dictionary

MY EXPERIENCE WITH THIS EMOTION:

I have eight grandchildren, which is a lot of love to give. I've changed my Instagram name several times to accommodate this ever-growing number of grandchildren — "Grammy007,"(this last number frequently changing to accommodate each new birth) and now the latest, "Eight Is Enough." I tell this story because being with my grandchildren makes me so happy. Six boys and two girls. When the first grandchild was born, I was intentional about what kind of Grammy I wanted to be. When they were little, I crawled, ran, danced and played with them. I can even remember doing cartwheels with them on my front yard. Well, it's been 13 years since the first one was born. My grandchildren are 13, 12, 11, 8, 7, 5, 4, and 2.

As my grandchildren moved into their teenage years, again I was intentional about having a relationship that would not become silent or distant as they entered puberty. I will not stand for the one word answers teenagers give to adults as we try ever-so-hard to communicate with them. The oldest four I usually spend Friday nights with. I pick them up to spend the night with me — and the journey, with a pit stop for pizza — takes almost two hours. During our drive time, I make it a practice to talk about what's going on with them. No electronic devices or gadgets…just our time to talk. We talk about basketball, football, what they want to be when they grow up, what kind of wife they want in their future and more.

I love these conversations and they make my heart melt. But the greatest happiness came during one of our Friday drives that one of my grandsons told me that a girl in school "threw it back" on him. I'm screaming inside, not knowing what that means, but trying to play it cool. So I asked, "what does that mean?" They all snicker and laugh and try to explain it to me. For me this is happiness at its best.

I had achieved what I intentionally set out to do. That night at Grammy's house, we talked about how to deal with inappropriate behavior that they are not interested in allowing it to persist. We actually did role play and of course, I was the "fast" girl in school. We had such a good time, but they learned valuable life skills.

HOW DID I MANAGE THIS EMOTION?

I allowed it to have its full expression and shared it with my grandson. Gut busting laughter filled the room as we continued to talk, laugh and even dance together that evening. It was wonderful!

HOW DID I MANAGE THE SOCIAL SETTING?

I created the environment where they could continue to share their life with me. I want them to feel like they can share anything with me. They always say, "Grammy's house is a house of love" and that again makes me happy.

LESSONS LEARNED FROM THIS EMOTION:

How important it is to be intentional in life. I can vividly remember the day I set this intention. I even asked my husband what kind of "Papa" he wanted to be. I wanted us both to create what I never had: a beautiful, healthy relationship with a grandmother. I don't even have that point of reference. However, I can say intention plus focus and consistent effort equals happiness.

IF FACED WITH THIS SITUATION AGAIN, WHAT WOULD I DO DIFFERENTLY:

Nothing. It's just the way I intended it to be.

My experience with this emotion:

How did I manage this emotion?

How did I manage the social setting?

Lessons learned from this emotion:

If faced with this situation again, what would I do differently:

REFLECTIONS

REFLECTIONS

INADEQUATE

Inadequate –"Not adequate, not capable."

- Merriam-Webster's Dictionary

MY EXPERIENCE WITH THIS EMOTION:

I'm a Leadership Coach and I must say I'm pretty darn good at what I do. I have trained over 7,000 individuals and have coached hundreds of leaders within different organizations including C-Suite leaders. Coaching is my sweet spot and helping others reach their full potential is my passion. Being in this space of discovery is electrifying for me.

I start with this intro because so many times when parenting my adult children, I feel inadequate. Ugh, it hurts to even write it, but I do. All of my experience in coaching seems to go out the window when it comes to my children. I immediately want to fix any problem or situation that arises. I remember fondly when their problems were, "I lost my jacket on the playground" or "I forgot my lunch." I can fix that and enjoy the look my children had when they felt like I could make everything okay.

Now my children are adults - 30, 32, and 34 - and their concerns are so much more complex. My 34-year-old daughter is a widow with three sons. My 32 -year-old son has been married for eleven years with two children and in an apprenticeship program, but his heart is screaming, "I'm an Entrepreneur." My 30-year-old daughter is married with three children and just graduated from nursing school and working the midnight shift. "Whew." Can you imagine the concerns, issues and conversations we have? As a coach I understand the value of questions. As a parent I know I should function as an advisor, but as a mom I want to fix it and make it all better. I can't fix their problems and often don't have the answers, so I feel inadequate. Not to mention, so many of their life experiences are very different from mine. When I was their age, my life mimicked my mom's life. I could look at her and have an idea of what to do and if that wasn't enough I could just ask her. I fondly remember her giving me advice based on her experience as a wife and mother that was very similar to my life. My oldest daughter (widow) is a single parent of three boys. "What advice do I give her?" I pray and ask for wisdom in the moment, but it still does not take away the feeling of inadequacy and wanting to take her pain away and make it alright.

My son wants to drop out of the apprenticeship program and become a Coach/ Entrepreneur. Even though that's exactly what I'm doing, I was raised by traditional parents and every morsel in my body is yelling, "Don't quit your steady job/paycheck for a dream!!!" My heart says, "go for it," so at this moment, I fall back to powerful coaching questions. Still not sure if this is the right road to take - INADEQUATE - there is that feeling again!

My youngest daughter is an RN who is trying to adjust to her new career. Working midnights/12 hour shifts and a toddler at home. I listen, my thoughts are, "I miss my mom. She too was a nurse, she could probably give great advice in this situation." My emotion… INADEQUATE.

I know some of you are reading this and you have the answers and you want to fix it for me. STOP. Be in this emotion with me because I have learned some valuable lessons, but let me share with you how I managed the social setting.

HOW DID I MANAGE THE SOCIAL SETTING:

I asked each of my children what they needed from me at this stage in their life. Which role would you like me to play in this conversation - advisor, coach, mom, friend, or just a good listener? The response would vary and I would adjust. Even writing about these conversations, that emotion still bubbles up, however, it is not as intense. I acknowledge and tell myself, "You don't have to fix it Cathy, you don't have to be perfect, you're doing just fine." That self assurance and love from myself calms me immensely. My level of listening increases and my need to fix decreases. At that moment, I feel equipped because I can bring all that I am to the conversation and a big part of who I am is their mom. I carried them in my belly for nine months, nursed them for 18 months, and I will love them for eternity. These experiences qualify me for the job of being their mom even though I sometimes feel inadequate. Like most moms would say, "This too shall pass."

LESSONS LEARNED FROM THIS EMOTION:

This emotion is okay because it causes me to ask questions within myself and with my children. It moves me to have and seek a deeper understanding of where I am as a mother and where they are as young adults. I've also learned that it's okay not to have all the answers, even though I believe my mom did and I guess, once again I'm trying to be like her. Big shoes to fill. I think I'm still in the midst of learning the lesson that it's okay to wear my own shoes.

IF FACED WITH THIS SITUATION AGAIN, WHAT WOULD I DO DIFFERENTLY:

Well, fortunately, I often have the opportunity to relive these moments with my children. I still find myself wanting to fix. I'm humanly imperfect and writing about it helps me to recall that I now play a different role. I guess I'm still practicing.

My experience with this emotion:

How did I manage this emotion?

How did I manage the social setting?

Lessons learned from this emotion:

If faced with this situation again, what would I do differently:

REFLECTIONS

INSIGHTFUL

Insightful –"Exhibiting or characterized by insight." Synonyms: Discerning, perceptive, prudent, sagacious, sage, wise.

- Merriam-Webster's Dictionary

MY EXPERIENCE WITH THIS EMOTION:

So the story about my relationship with my grandchildren was definitely intentional and because I spend a lot of time with my emotions and in a place of introspection, I often ask myself - "What is the relationship with my grandchildren all about? Is it deeper than what most grandparents feel?" For it truly is a different kind of love that most grandparents have for their grand babies. It appears they become different people when they have that first grandchild. Our children will readily say, "You never allowed us to do that!"

I used to look at my mom as an example of what a grandmother should be. She was my reference point because I did not have a grandmother who made a big fuss over me. My mother's mom died when I was just four years old. She would have been the one to adore me. I remember her frequent visits to our home. Every

time she came, she would bend over and give me a shiny quarter with a beautiful smile and her captivating green eyes. Everything about these moments were sparkly; her teeth, her smile, her eyes, and of course the shiny quarter.

I vividly remember those moments as I write. She was snatched from my life by a horrible car accident. My grandfather ran into a pole and she was thrown out of the car window. This was long before passengers were required to wear seat belts, as the story was told to me when I was much older. Of course, I didn't understand that at four years old, but I knew something was missing.

My dad's mother was her replacement and there was no special treatment from her. In fact, I often felt like she didn't like me at all. One day she actually told me that she didn't like the way I looked because of the color of my skin. As I grew older, my estimation was she had reflected her self-hatred onto me, because I look so much like her. I felt so empty and unloved in her presence. Especially because she did not treat my siblings the way she treated me. She was nicer to them. So fast forward to 2005 when I became a grandmother for the first time, I knew I wanted so much to have a loving, meaningful relationship with any and all grandchildren I would have. (Who knew it would be eight of them?) The emotion of being Insightful bubbles up and reaffirms that we are our childhood. I understand why I put so much effort into the relationships with my grandchildren. On the surface, it looks like its all for them, but Insight lets me know that a portion of it is me still healing from my childhood wounds - one grandmother gone too soon and the other grandmother's self-hatred.

HOW DID I MANAGE THIS EMOTION?

I sat in this emotion and learned the lesson. I allowed it to have it's full expression even though being in the space was sometimes painful. When I'm in the midst of painful emotions, I often remind myself that emotions rise and fall, they come and go and "this too shall pass," however, I do want to capture the knowledge found in this moment of being insightful.

HOW DID I MANAGE THE SOCIAL SETTING?

I shower my grandchildren with love and affection. We do all sorts of fun things. We sit in the " circle of love" with snacks and talk about our day. We gather around the fireplace and make s 'mores while we tell stories. We make costumes and act out bible characters. So many exciting and memorable experiences. I just love it! Possibly more than they do.

LESSONS LEARNED FROM THIS EMOTION:

Great things happen in the silence. I've learned that most of us are often reliving or running from our childhood. It's taking the time to sit with myself and meditate that I have insight into what's really behind the effort I put into loving "eight is enough." One grandmother gone too soon and the victim of the other grandmother's self-hatred. I'm no longer a victim, I'm a survivor with insight and intention to create the love for my grandchildren that I missed growing up.

IF FACED WITH THIS SITUATION AGAIN,
WHAT WOULD I DO DIFFERENTLY:

Nothing - it's better than I imagined!

My experience with this emotion:

How did I manage this emotion?

How did I manage the social setting?

Lessons learned from this emotion:

If faced with this situation again, what would I do differently:

REFLECTIONS

JEALOUSY

Jealousy –"Jealous resentment against a rival, a person enjoying success or advantage, etc., or against another's success or advantage itself."

- Dictionary.com

MY EXPERIENCE WITH THIS EMOTION:

While at *LA Fitness Total Body Workout* with a new instructor — who had the body of a goddess— jealousy reared its ugly head. Her movements were effortless and she included a lot of dance moves. I used to be a great dancer "back in the day" in my teens and 20s. Now as I get older, my mind still dances as I did in my teens and 20s but as I'm in the workout class surrounded by mirrors, I can't help but notice that my movements in my head don't match the movements I see in the mirror. I also notice that despite watching what I eat and exercising, I'm still a bit larger than I would like to be. As I gazed over to our instructor, who is bouncing, dancing, shaking and grooving to the beat, I feel insecure. Ugh. Painful. My natural inclination is to move out of it, especially in this environment. I need to keep up with the class, however, I stay there for a moment and insecurity eventually moves to jealousy. I name it, explore it, and plan to revisit it at home.

HOW DID I MANAGE THIS EMOTION?

One of the principles of Emotional Intelligence is being able to name an emotion in the moment and then validate it. Well, I've named it. Yep, it's jealousy and I recognize that validation typically lessens the intensity of the emotion. So, with love, tenderness and honesty, I began this process. "Cathy my dear, you have every reason to feel this way. Getting older is not always easy. My insecurities are …"Will I always be young, pretty, shapely, or is this the beginning of the end of my youth?" I've worked so hard up until this point. I don't know if I can work harder. I can, but do I want to?"

Later that evening when I arrived home, I gave myself a lot of self-love. I told myself, "Practice self-compassion Cathy, what would you tell a wounded friend who is feeling insecure? Place your hand over your heart look in the mirror and say it to yourself." I stood in the mirror and noticed everything I love about me and my body. I am well into my 50s with the shape of a 1930s Coca-Cola bottle. I can still rock a sleeveless t-shirt with arms that make my husband take a second glance. I know this for sure because he just commented on "the guns" a couple of days ago. And as far as my youth, it is a process of gracefully letting go and moving on to the next phase in my life. I've come to recognize that I get to determine when to make that transition and it doesn't have to happen in an aerobics class, which is only 50 minutes long. "Embrace who you are, Cathy…you're pretty amazing!" I managed this emotion with the self-love and the reassurance I needed to move through it.

HOW DID I MANAGE THE SOCIAL SETTING?

Two days later I attended the same class. After the workout, I approached the instructor telling her how much I enjoyed her music, her energy, and her dancing. She smiled brightly and said, "Oh thank you, I'm a dancer and I've always modeled myself after Richard Simmons." We laughed so hard because we're both African American women…Who would have thought either of us could be inspired by Richard Simmons?! Gut-busting laughter, encouragement, enthusiasm, and fun filled the room. What a blessing!

LESSONS LEARNED FROM THIS EMOTION:

Just think how different the outcome would have been if I had allowed jealousy to dominate and keep me from returning to class. What would have happened if I just repressed it and not listened? There was great value in listening and validating this emotion. It allowed me to come face-to-face with myself. Instead of pretending it doesn't exist, I learned that I could become my own cheerleader and give myself the security I needed. I realized it was this same voice that made me feel insecure and now I can intentionally in control it. I have the power to change the message and manage this emotion.

IF FACED WITH THIS SITUATION AGAIN, WHAT WOULD I DO DIFFERENTLY:

I'm not sure I would do anything differently. I was able to respond to this emotion instead of reacting and give myself the love and security I needed to allow jealousy to have its full expression.

My experience with this emotion:

How did I manage this emotion?

How did I manage the social setting?

Lessons learned from this emotion:

If faced with this situation again, what would I do differently:

REFLECTIONS

REFLECTIONS

LOVE

Love –"Love is patient and kind. Love is not jealous. It does not brag, does not get puffed up, does not behave indecently, does not look for its own interests, does not become provoked. It does not keep account of the injury. It does not rejoice over unrighteousness but rejoices with the truth. It bears all things, believes all things, hopes all things, endures all things. Love never fails."

- 1 Corinthians 13:4-8

MY EXPERIENCE WITH THIS EMOTION:

My experience with this emotion is when my husband of 36 years continues to "play" with me. I'm a child at heart and very creative by nature and of course, he is my opposite. He is the structured one in the relationship and tends to take a cautious approach to life. Initially, this felt restrictive to me. However, I have come to appreciate his consistent approach to life and the solid foundation he continues to provide in our relationship. In fact, it is because of his structure, he has given me wings to fly and has allowed me to soar higher than I ever thought I could (love is patient). He is very patient with me and I can feel his love for me.

So back to him "playing" with me… I love to take pictures that tell a story; in the moment as it is unfolding. I'm not fond of pictures where people pose and look into the camera. I want to capture moments that express the emotions as events are happening. Pictures are indeed worth a 1000 words. In order for me to do that, my husband has to stretch himself outside of his comfort zone and "play" with me. So for years now, I've been inviting him to join me in taking pictures in the moment. Initially, this was met with resistance and slight frustration from him, especially if he was in the middle of focusing on a task at hand and getting things done the right way on the first try. There were times when he was in the middle of handling leadership responsibilities, and I would approach him and ask him to "play" with me. He would push back or give me the, "Really? Are you kidding me?! Not right now," look. Well, for the past few years instead of him being solely focused on always handling business or checking things off his mental checklist, he has not only engaged in this creative picture taking, but he has started to enjoy it. Now, because of his willingness, capturing these moments takes very little effort and he has to learn to "play" the game with ease. These moments are so beautiful - (love hopes all things). I had always hoped he would come to enjoy capturing these special moments. When I look at these pictures, the emotion I feel is LOVE, because he has consistently stepped out of his comfort zone to make me happy (love does not look for its own interest). Creative picture taking is just a small part of our marriage, but it so represents our relationship on a much deeper level. So, please allow me to share our love story in slightly less than 1000 words.

We married and had children at a young age. My parents groomed my siblings and I for marriage and family life is a part of our heritage. As I mentioned in my gratitude story, my parents were married for 64 years, together for 70 years, childhood sweethearts. So all of my siblings and I followed in their footsteps. Looking back, I recognize because I married at a young age I missed the opportunity to get know who I was as an individual before I joined my husband on this life long journey called marriage. What we did know at 18 and 21, was that we were in love, but more than likely blinded to the realities that marriage would bring. Yes, on our wedding day, July 30, 1983, our names were Tony and Cathy, but they would quickly be changed to mommy and daddy before we even knew who Tony and Cathy were as adults. We would go on to raise our three beautiful children and enjoy being married for many years until I entered what some call "middle age."

My mid-30s proved to be a very difficult time for me as I have previously written about in my story about Depression. The time had come for me to figure out who I was as an individual in this marriage and at the same time, being a mom. Yes, because I married at 18 and had a baby at 19, 21, and 23, I didn't have time to figure out who I was as an adult. I can remember one day my youngest daughter looked at my diploma and did the math, and asked me a very profound question, "Dang, mommy, what happened to your youth?" That question felt like a punch in my chest. I knew the answer to that question, but I was on a quest to find the answer to other questions that were more pressing to me at this moment — "Who am I? What do I really like to do? What fills me up?" Because I didn't know who I was at this time, I wasn't in love with myself. I could only treat my mate the way I treated myself so I did not always show up in a loving way. Looking back, I could have done a better job of communicating what I wanted during this time. However, the problem was...I did not always know what I wanted. I probably could have been kinder, but I was angry inside and did not know it- (love is patient). Applying the principles of what LOVE really is, I eventually worked through the discomfort of welcoming the new and improved Cathy into our marriage - (love endures all things).

Fast forward, to where we are today, I'm in my 50s and I'm so happy to be with someone who genuinely loves me. He has seen the good, the bad and the ugly side of me and he is still in love with me. My husband and I have grown up together, and have raised three beautiful children. We have been empty nesters for 10 years, and I have to say it is absolutely amazing! Love at 18 and 21 years of age is giddy, exciting, and physical. However, love at this stage in our marriage for me is all-encompassing - it is physical, spiritual, mental, and emotional. It is spiritual because I recognize that he is my spiritual head and I love it when he takes the lead in this way. It is emotional when I recognize him working so hard to validate my emotions and sit in the silence with me and/or just listen. Again, this is not who he is by nature… remember he is facts-driven and he is a man who wants to jump in and fix the problem. He knows when to put his tool belt away and allow me to talk as he patiently listens (love does not look for its own interest). He has also been my biggest cheerleader in writing this book and for that, I am so grateful. There have been many times that I have needed his emotional support to continue on this journey of

recanting so many past experiences. Some were painful. It's also mental because just as I have been on this continuous journey of growth and development, so has he. There are times during our conversations where my mind is saying, "Who is this man? He's so intriguing. I like him and I'm glad he's mine." I have also watched him shift from not knowing who he was, to defining his identity and transforming into to the man he is today into the man he wants to become. After 36 years, we're still getting to know each other as we purposely evolve into better individuals and become better marriage mates. I believe this growth process will continue throughout our marriage - (love believes all things).

HOW DID I MANAGE THIS EMOTION?

I love Love! I don't need to manage this emotion. I allow it to have its full expression. I'm very big on speaking organically from the heart and soul in our relationship and frequently expressing how much I love him. I think if there is anything about this emotion that needs to be managed, it is to make sure it continues to grow with meaningful communication being the key.

HOW DID I MANAGE THE SOCIAL SETTING?

I feel so blessed to have learned the value of open-ended questions, and how to go beneath the surface during our conversations. I've been able to ask insightful questions to find out what love means to him; and when he shares these things, I try hard to respond because I want him to know how much I love him. His love language is "acts of service." One way I express my love language towards him is to pack him a nice home-cooked meal so that when he opens his lunch at work he can be proud of his wife's abilities in the kitchen and feel loved at the same time. It's the little things that mean a lot.

IF FACED WITH THIS SITUATION AGAIN, WHAT WOULD I DO DIFFERENTLY:

There were times when I wish that I had not married so young. Even when our own children wanted to marry young, we tried to encourage them to wait. But what did they say to us? "You guys married young!" Our response was, "That's why we can tell you to wait!" This didn't mean that we didn't love each other, this meant that we were living the reality of marriage and parenting at a young age. I think it is important to really know who you are as an individual - know your strengths and your weaknesses so that you can choose someone that will complement your weaknesses. My husband and I had to grow up while raising kids. Even though we did, it was not without discomfort - (love does not keep account of the injury). However, I would do it all over again because I love our life together now. This stage in our marriage is better than the honeymoon stage. We genuinely know who we are as individuals and we work hard to bring the best of who we are to this wonderful arrangement called marriage which is indeed based on love.

LESSONS LEARNED FROM THIS EMOTION:

I have learned to walk and live in the definition of love even when it is uncomfortable. I think because of movies, love songs and everything we see in society that we often think of love, in terms of how we want to feel in the relationship, we only want to be the receiver. I know I did initially. Remember, I'm the baby of six and used to being spoiled, so why should this relationship be any different. When it came to my husband and I, in my mind it was truly all about me. As I matured, my outlook changed and I begin to really recognize how frequently he was stepping out of his comfort zone to demonstrate his love for me. I eventually realized that I had to learn the true meaning of love and what was most critical for me to grasp - (love does not look for its own interest).

Reading the definition of this emotion, and living by it, are two different things. Sometimes it is not always easy to not look for my own interests, or not become provoked, or not to keep account of the injury, however, if you look closely, this definition comes with a guarantee, "Love never fails." This is indeed the lesson I have learned over the past 36 years.

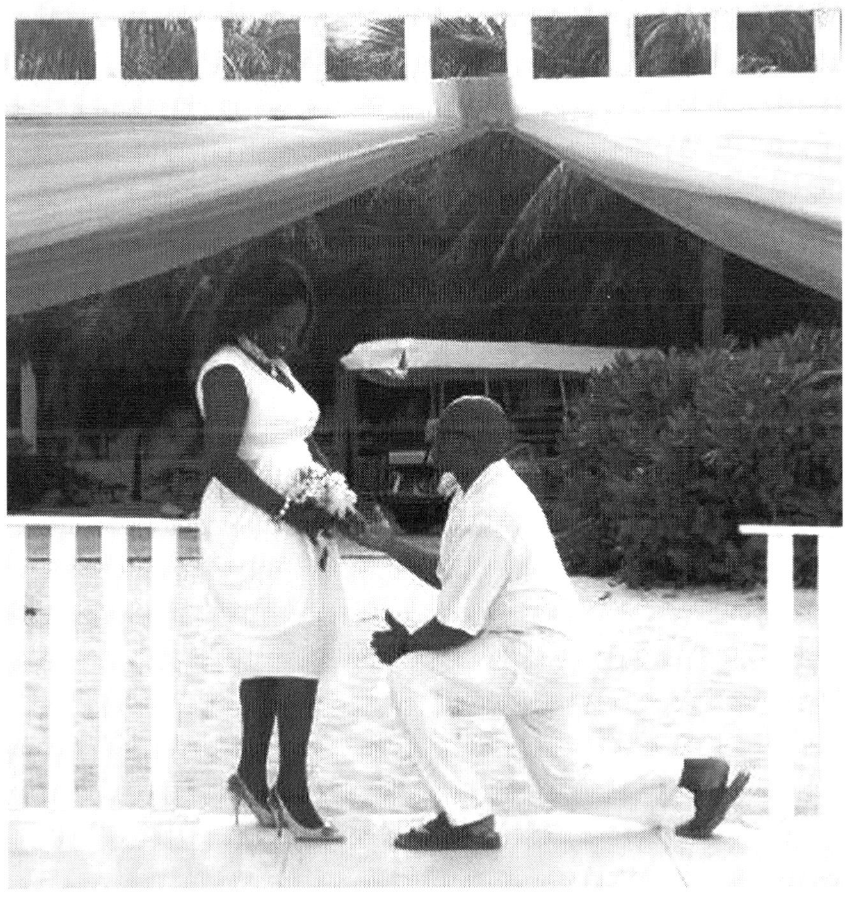

My experience with this emotion:

How did I manage this emotion?

How did I manage the social setting?

Lessons learned from this emotion:

If faced with this situation again, what would I do differently:

REFLECTIONS

REFLECTIONS

NUMB

Numb –"Unable to think, feel or react normally because of something that shocks or upsets you."

- Merriam-Webster's Dictionary

MY EXPERIENCE WITH THIS EMOTION:

Recently one of my close friends reached out to me and said, "I need to talk." She invited another close friend because the dynamics of this relationship always includes the three of us. When she arrived at my house, Kendra wasn't there. She would end up being 90 minutes late.

It was a Monday night and I needed to get up early for work. I told Michelle upon her arrival that I needed to go to bed at 11:00 pm so our girlfriend time had a limit on it this night. At 10:00 pm, Michelle and I had been just chit-chatting. I said, "What is it you want to talk about?" She said, "I can't tell you yet, I have to wait until Kendra arrives. I want to tell the two of you together." She said we should all be devastated at the same time. From my perspective, Michelle is a tower of strength. She would be the "Olivia Pope" of this three-way friendship, so whatever her news was that she wanted to share, I assumed it had something to do with her kids, grandkids, or her job.

Kendra arrived two hours late in her camouflage jeans, her big personality, ready to dropkick the world. I call her my Shero. So we laugh and talk, get loud and hug, and then Michelle says, "Okay, I have something tell you guys…I have breast cancer." At this moment I was literally numb. Ever so conscious that I needed to support my friend, I'm not sure what emotion showed on my face but internally I know I felt numb. Everything from this moment seemed like a bad movie playing in slow motion, with us as the three main characters. Kendra teared up and cried (my Shero). Her drop-kicking enthusiasm has shifted to fear and sorrow. I looked over to comfort her giving her permission to cry and feel what she feels. As I intently focus on Shero, I again go inside to notice what I feel and again the answer is "numb." We all began to support one another with a group hug. I began to think of my mom who was initially diagnosed with breast cancer in 1996 and later died of lung cancer in 2014.

From there I think of my best friend from childhood who died at the young age of 38 from breast cancer. We were friends for 30 years. We met in our congregation and attended elementary school together. She, too, was taken from me too soon. After these thoughts, I again drop down into my heart to check for an emotion and what I do feel is a little door that closes over my heart for protection that will not allow me to process or feel. So the emotion I again feel is numb!

HOW DID I MANAGE THIS EMOTION?

I'm not sure I did manage it. It had its full expression during this moment of devastating news. I didn't share this feeling with my friends because I didn't think it would help or comfort, so I kept it inside. I guess to some degree I did manage it. Maybe?

HOW DID I MANAGE THE SOCIAL SETTING?

I hug Michelle as tight as I can, but my heart isn't there. I hold Shero's hand and tell her it's okay to cry. The two of them cry.

I watch and support, saying all the right things. "We're going to be okay." Shero says, "I'll take you to your doctors' appointments," I say nothing at this moment. I've been down this road before with my mom sitting through chemo and with my friend, wheeling her into the bathroom to throw up right after chemo. I'm silent because I believe fear and trepidation creeps in and that door over my heart now seems to seal itself with weatherproofing and a deadbolt lock. I'm afraid to open it.

IF FACED WITH THIS SITUATION AGAIN, WHAT WOULD I DO DIFFERENTLY:

I would probably share my feelings with my friends. I don't like going through the motions of "saying the right things," or giving hugs with a heart that is locked away. Sharing this emotion would allow my love and support to be more authentic. I did not want this moment to be about me externally, but on the inside, I was truly protecting myself. Looking back, I think the friendship we have is a safe and appropriate place to share how I'm truly feeling. If faced with this again, (which I hope is not the case) I would open my heart and authentically share what I'm feeling in the moment.

LESSONS LEARNED FROM THIS EMOTION:

I think I have learned to have more empathy for people who numb themselves to their emotions in general because of repeated hurt and disappointment in life. I know I will eventually unlock the door to my heart that is only trying to protect me. In this space of empathy, I validate this emotion of being numb for myself and will look for other opportunities to validate others when I'm sitting face-to-face with someone who is numb from fear of intense pain. Empathy is the lesson I've learned.

My experience with this emotion:

How did I manage this emotion?

How did I manage the social setting?

Lessons learned from this emotion:

If faced with this situation again, what would I do differently:

REFLECTIONS

NURTURED

Nurtured –"Care for and encourage growth and development."

- Merriam-Webster's Dictionary

MY EXPERIENCE WITH THIS EMOTION:

It's early morning just before sunrise. I've brewed my favorite cup of coffee. I'm preparing for my morning routine of Self Care. I have to hurry because I don't want to miss the actual rising of the sun.

I have a designated space in my home where I sit to watch the sunrise and look at the beautiful flowers planted by the owners of a restaurant nearby. This is my connection with nature and my Creator. I'm surrounded by my journal, my Bible, candles, essential oils and a blanket. Ahhhh. I think I have everything I need.

It's typically quiet in this space, it's about an hour before the rest of the world starts their morning. No cars, no people toiling about, just....silence. I love it!

I settle myself in my chair and I hear the geese quacking. Did you know that the one who quacks is the cheerleader of the group?

Then, I think about the Creator's personality and smile because I see a similarity in His creation within myself, as I'm a cheerleader by nature. With a smile on face, serenity in my heart, and my freshly-brewed cup of coffee in my hand, I see the sunrise peak above the restaurant behind my house. To me, it's like a grand production of *Phantom of the Opera*. I watch this repeat production of the sunrise every morning with great anticipation. Even though I know it's coming, its the same, yet different, each morning. The different shades and hues of orange, blues, and yellows are phenomenal.

I sit in silence and I don't move...only sip coffee. Watching this nurtures my soul and my spirit.

After the sunrise, I move to prayer. So much to be thankful for, many requests to refine my personality and infuse knowledge and wisdom into my heart and soul.

From here I pick up my Bible and begin to read. I have a vivid imagination that allows me to feel like I'm crossing the Red Sea with Moses and the Israelites. I can hear the waters standing congealed, and I can feel the sand on my feet. At this moment I feel NURTURED. My cup runneth over!

HOW DID I MANAGE THIS EMOTION?

I sit in this moment and cherish it. This is now my time for meditation. I truly have been cared for, encouraged, and developed on a mental, physical, spiritual and emotional level.

I allow it to have its full expression. I'm quiet, and I am listening.

HOW DID I MANAGE THE SOCIAL SETTING:

At this moment, I feel one with my Creator. I linger in prayer and thanksgiving for the beautiful gifts I'm able to find in creation every day. I'm in a place of deep gratitude with Him. I'm intentionally fully present and feel no need to rush out of the space.

LESSONS LEARNED FROM THIS EMOTION:

"Great things happen in the silence."

IF FACED WITH THIS SITUATION AGAIN, WHAT WOULD I DO DIFFERENTLY:

I am happy that I'm able to do this over and over again, every day. I've been doing this for almost 20 years. What would I do differently? I would have started this a lot earlier in life.

My experience with this emotion:

How did I manage this emotion?

How did I manage the social setting?

Lessons learned from this emotion:

If faced with this situation again, what would I do differently:

REFLECTIONS

REFLECTIONS

OFFENDED

Offended –"To cause (a person or group) to feel hurt, angry or upset by something said or done."

- Merriam-Webster's Dictionary

MY EXPERIENCE WITH THIS EMOTION:

My experience with this emotion happened shortly after I received a promotion into a leadership role at a large organization. It was my first of many meetings that would take place in the executive boardroom. Another African American woman and I were standing in the boardroom, excited to be there and ready to take on any organizational challenges and responsibilities that would be assigned to all who attended this meeting. However, what happens next is shocking and hurtful to me. One of the vice presidents walks into the boardroom and sees the two of us standing there in navy blue suits and this leader said, "You two look like flight attendants!" At that moment I was indeed offended. Not that I have anything against being a flight attendant (for it was my dream job at 18) - however, decades later I'm standing in a boardroom and not on an airplane and I'm viewed as someone in the service industry? I was indeed offended!

HOW DID I MANAGE THIS EMOTION?

There was a lot of internal dialogue in my head – "Oh no she didn't, how could she, there are other people in here wearing navy blue suits, why didn't she say that to them?" I'm offended! However, at some point I calmed myself down enough to pay attention. But I'm still angry and if I go deeper, I'm hurt. When will I ever be perceived as equal - I'm not sure if in the moment that I'm managing it well. I tried to pay attention, but as I write I can't even tell you what the meeting was about, but I can certainly feel the pain attached to that moment.

HOW DID I MANAGE THE SOCIAL SETTING?

I continued to sit in the meeting in and out of concentration because of the dialogue in my head. After the meeting, I asked this executive if I could have a moment of her time to speak with her in private. I recreated the moments in the boardroom for her and leading up to the comment that she made. I explained to her my enthusiasm and how happy I was to be a part of this team and to assume my new role. I also articulated clearly how her comments made me feel "less than" and not "equal to" all in the room. She immediately apologized. I asked her "What was it that made you see us as flight attendants?" She said uncomfortably, "It was the blue suits." I pointed out that others in the room had on blue suits. She again apologized profusely and we were able to have an open dialogue about my feelings as an African American woman in that space and how her comments were perceived. I feel like this was a very candid conversation that actually improved our relationship.

IF FACED WITH THIS SITUATION AGAIN, WHAT WOULD I DO DIFFERENTLY:

I wouldn't change a thing. I think I managed this emotion and social setting well. I continued to work for this organization for quite some time and with this particular executive. I'm grateful for the growth opportunities that I was afforded and I still have a relationship with this individual I wouldn't change a thing. Looking back I'm proud of how I handled the situation.

LESSONS LEARNED FROM THIS EMOTION:

I may not ever be able to change people's perception of me no matter where I'm standing, whether in a boardroom or on an airplane. I've learned that people have their own set of biases and life experiences that make them uniquely their own. Being courageous enough to have the crucial conversation was empowering. However, what was most rewarding was creating an awareness in the work environment that small consistent comments can create an environment of micro-inequities. If this behavior is left unchecked over a period of time, it can create a culture that makes individuals question their equality, their abilities, and cause them to disengage. It's been said that "culture change happens one conversation at a time." I hope this was one of those conversations that evoked change.

My experience with this emotion:

How did I manage this emotion?

How did I manage the social setting?

Lessons learned from this emotion:

If faced with this situation again, what would I do differently:

REFLECTIONS

REFLECTIONS

SAD

Sad –"Affected with or expressive of grief or unhappiness."

- Merriam-Webster's Dictionary

MY EXPERIENCE WITH THIS EMOTION:

It was a Friday night, the night I usually spend with my grandsons. I was in the kitchen sweeping the floor. My eight-year-old grandson Noah came up from the basement to ask me, "Grammy is there anything I can do to help you?" My heart melted in this moment, so indeed I said, "You can help me sweep the floor." He excitedly grabs the broom and begins to sweep. I smiled as I watch him, thinking to myself how adorable he is. A few minutes pass by and then he stops, looks at me and says, "Grammy if you're still alive when I have kids, what will you be to them?" It is in this moment that I experienced the emotion of being sad.

I'm sure you're probably wondering why? His question — "If I'm still alive when he has kids" — reminds me that he has experience death one too many times in his eight years of life. Just two and a half years ago he lost his dad and five years ago he lost his GG — his great-grandmother, my mother, so yes, his question saddens me.

HOW DID I MANAGE THIS EMOTION?

Internally I validated this emotion for myself by being insightful and understanding his vantage point. I felt no need to take this conversation to a sad place. It's amazing how two people can be in the same moment and experience it differently. However, I kept this moment as Noah intended it to be for him, which was a happy moment as he exhibits childlike curiosity. So of course, you know the questions keep coming.

HOW DID I MANAGE THE SOCIAL SETTING?

"I then responded to his question and said, "I'll be their great grandmother." Noah then says, "Ohhhh, like GG?" (that's what he called my mother.) He then said with excitement in his voice and brightness in his eyes "And my mommy will be their Grammy right?" I said to him, "Yes Noah that's right!" It was indeed a beautiful moment to see him make the connections.

IF FACED WITH THIS SITUATION AGAIN, WHAT WOULD I DO DIFFERENTLY:

Nothing, this moment is just what it needs it to be.

LESSONS LEARNED FROM THIS EMOTION:

The reason for my initial sadness was because I was 40 years old before I lost someone dear to me. Noah's young heart had already been broken twice at the tender age of eight. However, in this moment I saw that he was indeed healing. There was no sadness on his face or in his voice, for him it was just an inquisitive question. My lesson learned is our hearts do eventually heal. However, when we are in the midst of a tragedy we feel like they never will. For about a year-and-a-half after Noah's dad died, Noah was the one who would look at pictures and say, "I miss my daddy." He would often burst out crying and lay in his mother's arms for quite a while. He is a very emotionally expressive child and this was a difficult journey for him. So to see him in this space today of childlike curiosity shows me that both of our hearts are healing.

My experience with this emotion:

How did I manage this emotion?

How did I manage the social setting?

Lessons learned from this emotion:

If faced with this situation again, what would I do differently:

REFLECTIONS

REFLECTIONS

SPECIAL

Special –"Readily distinguishable from others of the same category; held in particular esteem."

- Merriam-Webster's Dictionary

MY EXPERIENCE WITH THIS EMOTION:

I've been reading about how having electronic devices in the bedroom is probably not the best for healthy sleep habits. I have long banned the TV from our bedroom years ago. Hubby wasn't happy. So now I've taken it to the next level. It has become very personal for me. No cell phone in bed, or iPad. I've finally established a healthy bedtime routine: Facial and skin care, brush my teeth, soft cuddly pajamas and lavender *Young Living* essential oil. Once I'm in bed, it takes me quite some time to fall asleep and in this moment I feel very special. As I replay my day in my head, I'm so pleased that I have taken care of myself mentally (reading or learning something new), spiritually (prayer, Bible reading, meditation), physically (body works and abs), emotionally (journaling-coaching, connecting with others). A smile crosses my face...my heart is full and warm, and I feel loved and cared for by myself. I've made myself a priority and it feels pretty special to me.

HOW DID I MANAGE THIS EMOTION?

Just be in this moment, applaud myself and offer a prayer of gratitude.

HOW DID I MANAGE THE SOCIAL SETTING?

This is a moment shared with my Heavenly Father. I offer a prayer of thanksgiving and relish the time and space with Him. I highly esteem this moment.

LESSONS LEARNED FROM THIS EMOTION:

I truly understand the meaning behind "Love your neighbor as you love yourself." Because I feel special, I so enjoy making others feel special, too. I have truly experienced the truthfulness of "there is more happiness in giving than receiving." I truly have much to give as I enjoy this moment. This healthy bedtime routine has been such an eye-opener.

IF FACED WITH THIS SITUATION AGAIN, WHAT WOULD I DO DIFFERENTLY:

I wouldn't change a thing. I wish I would have arrived at this point much sooner in life. In my blog, brewingcoffeewithcathy.com. I've written about my early 20s and 30s where I was always depleted, feeling empty and in the bowels of depression. Now, well into my 50s, I can confidently say, I wouldn't change a thing about this moment.

My experience with this emotion:

How did I manage this emotion?

How did I manage the social setting?

Lessons learned from this emotion:

If faced with this situation again, what would I do differently:

REFLECTIONS

SQUASHED

Squashed –"To put down, suppress."

- Merriam-Webster's Dictionary

MY EXPERIENCE WITH THIS EMOTION:

I was working with a large organization for 13 years and I loved my role in this organization. I was helping to lead a culture change initiative where I would eventually train over 3,500 individuals (including the entire executive team along with board members). This training took place over an eight-year period.

Our culture did indeed change! This organization began to create amazing customer service experiences and the employees, for the most part, began to function as a family. It was electrifying to be part of this transformational change. An integral part of this culture change also included coaching many of the leaders.

I mention this because I had such a wonderful leader who supported my growth and development so that when an opportunity came along for me to receive formal education as an executive coach, she allowed me to participate. We were in her office one day and she said, "There's only one spot available in this training. I can go, but, because this is your passion, I can step back and allow you to attend." I was so excited! She was always interested and very in-tune to my growth and development. She was also keenly aware of my natural gifts and talents and she intentionally put me in spaces and places where I could use them for the good of our team and the organization as a whole. I grew tremendously under her leadership. Thank you, Toni Flowers!

Well, the time came for this leader to exit the organization to pursue her personal dreams. Her departure left a void in my heart and had the potential to stop my professional growth and development. After she left, I was given a large part of her work to manage, and I realized that I would have to be responsible and look out for my own growth and development and make things happen for myself, and I did!

I love learning and took every certification and training class that became available within the organization. Meanwhile, I was also enjoying the privilege of the new function in my role as an executive coach for many leaders in the organization. My new responsibilities included traveling to other states to coach executives and their teams. Out of all the roles I fulfilled in this organization, coaching was my sweet spot. It's my passion and it's like breathing to me.

A few months later, I was offered a promotion, which would include leading an entire department. However, this wasn't an easy decision because I was concerned about getting a new boss and wondering if they would be able to lead me effectively. I was also interested in continuing my journey as an executive coach. I knew this new role would absorb a lot of my time, therefore, I decided not to accept this offer.

My decline meant that the organization would hire someone else for this leadership role. From the day she arrived, I knew things would be different. Oh, I expected that. I also understood that she would need time to get acclimated to her new environment. However, as time went by, I did not feel as though I would be able to grow under her leadership.

There are several incidents that took place where I felt like we were just oil and water and that we were never going to mix. Our communication styles were vastly different. Her style was very information and data-driven while I was at the opposite end of the spectrum when it comes to communication - all about people, experiences, and emotions.

This indeed proved to be a challenge in itself, because a large part of our culture change initiative had been spent on building relationships. I'm also a certified "Crucial Conversations" facilitator and I was excited to put into practice the principles of the training. I set out to have several crucial conversations with this leader about our relationship. I even used the YouTube video *"It's Not About the Nail,"* (https://www.youtube.com/watch?v=-4EDhdAHrOg) to show how different our communication styles were, and why we were having problems communicating effectively. Nothing from my perspective was working. The final straw was when she delivered the message that the organization was shifting their priorities in another direction that would not allow me to continue to function as a leadership coach. I was devastated and began to feel squashed!

HOW DID I MANAGE THIS EMOTION?

Before I can talk about how I managed it, let me share with you that there were a lot of other emotions that were mixed in with this emotion. I can name just a few:

Anger (because of no more coaching); Regret (for not taking the job); Irritation (because she wasn't my old boss, which was so unfair to her); and Frustration (that my old boss had left the organization).

As you can see, I was experiencing a plethora of emotions. But after sitting in the silence, the one that was eating at my gut was the feeling of being squashed (crushed and squeezed without support) with no freedom to continue to grow. I continued to journal daily about all of these emotions and validated each and every one of them along the way. There's something so powerful about being able to validate your own emotions when needed. It helped to think logically as I began to consider what would I do. I knew I could not stay in this space.

HOW DID I MANAGE THE SOCIAL SETTING?

Shortly after, I still had a mentor coach at the time, so I would use my next coaching session to discuss what I wanted to do about this situation. I knew I had a decision to make and I felt like I needed to leave this organization. In leadership development training we often say, "People don't leave organizations, they leave bosses." I had loved working at this organization for years but felt like I needed to exercise my option. I also talked it over with my husband, who on many days allowed me to vent and then asked appropriate questions that allowed me to think more logically. On some days this is exactly what I needed.

Fortunately, I had another coaching session and my coach asked me a very powerful question around leaving the organization. I will never forget this question or how I felt at the moment. She said, "What do you really want to do?" I said, "Jump!!!" She said, "Maybe that word 'jump' doesn't serve you…what would happen if you just leaned into the discomfort of leaving the organization, what would that be like for you?"

At that moment I could visually see in my mind the difference between jumping and leaning. Jumping to me meant that I didn't know where I was going to land and the end result is out of my control. Leaning into the discomfort made me feel like I was in control. When leaning, my feet are on the ground and I could always pull back if I leaned in too far, which means that I still have a measure of control. All of this happened internally in a matter of seconds. (Thank you Pat Barlow.) My response to her question was, "If I am just leaning into discomfort, I would be in control with my feet on the ground." After that coaching conversation, I typed out my resignation and turned it in that day!

IF FACED WITH THIS SITUATION AGAIN, WHAT WOULD I DO DIFFERENTLY:

Looking back I wouldn't change a thing. I love that I didn't constantly complain about a bad boss. I'm proud that I had several crucial conversations and I wasn't talking behind her back, but instead was talking to her. I've also learned that every emotion I felt was valuable - discomfort and being uncomfortable was valuable and has continued to mold and shape who I am today. If I had it to do all over again, I don't think I would do anything different.

LESSONS LEARNED FROM THIS EMOTION:

Growth happens when we are uncomfortable. I'm not even sure this boss was indeed a "bad boss." I just needed something different. It was not a good fit for either of us. Opting to leave the organization has resulted in my tremendous growth and development. I'm living my dream as an executive coach, consultant, facilitator and now if you are reading this book I am an Author. I would never have even imagined that I would ever have become an author! I'm not sure these things would have happened had I stayed with that organization. I can truly look back with gratitude in experiencing the emotion of feeling squashed, it has given me the freedom to stand tall, spread my wings and soar!

My experience with this emotion:

How did I manage this emotion?

How did I manage the social setting?

Lessons learned from this emotion:

If faced with this situation again, what would I do differently:

REFLECTIONS

REFLECTIONS

TIRED

Tired –"Exhausted, as by exertion, fatigued or sleepy."

- Merriam-Webster's Dictionary

MY EXPERIENCE WITH THIS EMOTION:

I'm literally in this emotion as I write this. My feet hurt, my back hurts. I have had back to back-to-back Leadership Development training sessions for the past three days, and these were eight-hour classes. I have nothing left to give. No cell phone, no TV - I feel zapped of energy…Yes, tired and exhausted!

HOW DID I MANAGE THIS EMOTION?

I'm listening to my body. I'm writing in bed in spite of physical exhaustion. I take a moment to validate this emotion. "You have every right to feel this way Cathy, you've given a lot in the last three days." Before coming home I treated myself to a nice dinner, a glass of wine, and have given myself permission to rest. Guilt-free R & R. I'm actively engaging in different things that I know will replenish me.

HOW DID YOU MANAGE THE SOCIAL SETTING?

In this setting it's just me, myself and I. I'm reflectively sitting in the silence, listening to what this emotion wants to convey. I've been here before and here I am again. I reflect on how I used to facilitate three days, eight-hour classes every week for eight years. It was a breeze. What has changed? The response that bubbles up for this question is…"You're older now Cathy. That was literally 10 years ago." My mind heart and soul says to me. "You need to take better care of us." I notice my breath quickens and my chest rises and falls at a quicker pace. The next question I ask myself is…"Will you?" I'm face to face with myself once again, and I have to be truthful. The honest answer is..."I certainly hope so, be patient with me Cathy, I'm a work in progress. "

IF FACED WITH THIS SITUATION AGAIN, WHAT WOULD I DO DIFFERENTLY?

Maybe a bubble bath. I'm too tired to run the water, to wait for the tub to fill, to sit long enough to enjoy it. As I really explore, write and listen to this emotion, I could set limits on how many days in a row I will facilitate. I still love what I do, but I think two days in a row is my limit for training and facilitating. That 's what I would do differently moving forward.

LESSONS LEARNED FROM THIS EMOTION:

"There is more happiness in giving than in receiving" is one of my values. So my lesson is, in order for me to feel that happiness that comes from giving, I need to have something to give. It's painful giving from an empty vessel. I have to set boundaries and recognize my limitations. I need to give myself permission to say "No" and love myself enough to be comfortable in hearing myself say this powerful two letter word. "No." When I say "No" to things that stretch me beyond my boundaries and physical limitations, I'm actually saying "Yes" to myself and I'm worth it.

As I sip, rest, reflect and write, my mind, soul, and spirit applauds me and my body feels better. I'm reminded of the power, beauty and my passion for self-care. I feel validated and loved by me.

My experience with this emotion:

How did I manage this emotion?

How did I manage the social setting?

Lessons learned from this emotion:

If faced with this situation again, what would I do differently:

REFLECTIONS

REFLECTIONS

VALIDATED

Validated –"To recognize, establish, or illustrate the worthiness or legitimacy of."

- Merriam-Webster's Dictionary

MY EXPERIENCE WITH THIS EMOTION:

Earlier in my book I wrote about the emotion of feeling inadequate at parenting adult children. I've truly experienced how emotions come and go - they rise and fall and based on what we do with them, they can bring us value or be disruptive if we ignore them for too long. So the emotion of feeling inadequate was soon replaced with the rewarding emotion of "validation."

This emotion was a result of my children expressing their gratitude to me, unsolicited out of the clear blue sky. My oldest daughter is my travel assistant and we check in with each other frequently throughout the week via email. One day I sent her an email with a travel request, and after fulfilling that request she sent me the following email:

"I got busy at work but was thinking about you this morning and how blessed I am to have a mother like you. I was thinking about how right after Steve died you would come over on my meeting night and make dinner and get the boys ready for the meeting. I will never forget that nor stop appreciating it. Thank you so, much for loving and supporting me through all this craziness. Love you!"

Shortly after that, my son sent me such a beautiful text. Months ago, I was traveling for business and I stopped at a Cracker Barrel in Louisville, Kentucky. I love stopping there not only for the food but they always have the cutest little gifts. I saw this little book entitled, "To My Son." The book had quotes and stories in it that were particular to a mother and son relationship. I went through the book over a period of three months, one page at a time, and wrote a personalized note on each page. My notes specifically spoke to the relationship my son and I have.

One day he dropped by, and I presented it to him with a few other little trinkets. I told him I think about him often and wanted to create a way he would consistently know that I was always thinking of him. I also suggested that he put this book under the seat of his car so that he would always have access to it whenever he needed a pick-me-up. He was so surprised and so appreciative of such a thoughtful gift. He said, "it's so beautiful to know that someone has been thinking about you over a period of time, enough where they would go through the pages of a book and write something special for you." Shortly after giving him this book, he sent me such a beautiful text expressing his gratitude. I again feel validated!

About two weeks later, my youngest daughter who is a registered nurse called to ask me to lunch after working a midnight shift. I'm so excited! We went to a nice restaurant and as we were sitting across the table from each other she asked, "I want your advice on something, I need your help." My heart was so excited and full of validation, I wanted to burst. Internally the conversation in my head was, "They still need me, just in a different way."

At this moment, I had to calm down so that I could listen to her request for help. She wanted to know how to settle her children down after they arrived home from school. This, I could readily give sound advice on. I could draw from my experience and also all of the wisdom my mother poured into me. At this moment I'm feeling so validated.

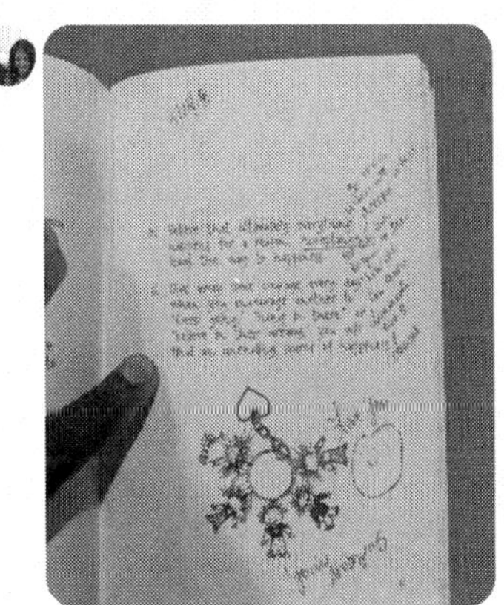

Was having a really tough day emotionally this book has really been helpful in so many ways. Thank you again

HOW DID I MANAGE THIS EMOTION?

I allowed myself to feel it internally, but I did not want to make this moment about me, so internally I validated this emotion and set it aside so that I could be fully present for my daughter. However, after our lunch together and on my drive home, I allowed this emotion its full expression. If I could describe this emotion, it felt like hot fudge being poured all over an ice cream sundae. It is all over my chest and makes my heart feel warm inside. This emotion and its full expression have nurtured not only my heart but my soul and spirit as well.

HOW DID I MANAGE THE SOCIAL SETTING?

I listened intently to my daughter and gave her what she later said was good advice and that it was working tremendously well. With my son, I immediately responded to his text with a heart full of joy.

Here is the text I sent him:

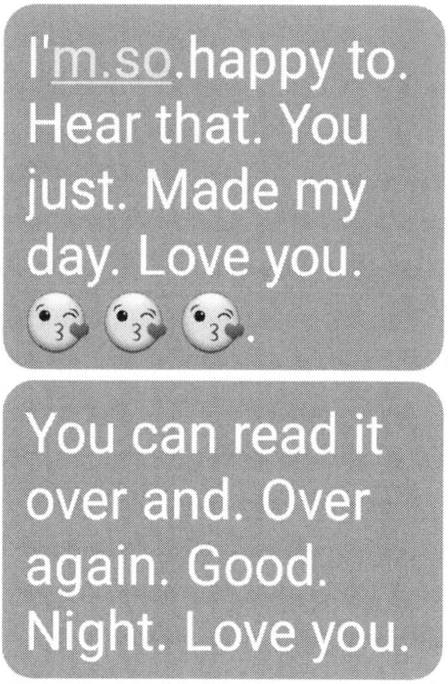

I'm.so.happy to. Hear that. You just. Made my day. Love you. 😘😘😘.

You can read it over and. Over again. Good. Night. Love you.

I also responded to my daughter via email and I will share that with you as well.

Here is my email response to my daughter:

> *"Awwwwww...that means so much to me. I always wonder if I'm doing enough and if I'm getting it right as a mother. Thank you so much. This feels like a million dollars to me."*

So I guess in managing the social setting one word that comes to mind is that I managed it with a heart full of gratitude.

IF FACED WITH THIS SITUATION AGAIN,
WHAT WOULD I DO DIFFERENTLY:

These moments are perfect the way they are. I have captured them not only on paper but also in my heart and soul. I love being a mom!

LESSONS LEARNED FROM THIS EMOTION:

One of the tenants of the principles of emotional intelligence is the power of validating emotions. Living in this space of being validated by my children really impresses upon me the need to listen to others and validate their emotions. I've also learned that just because I sometimes feel inadequate as a parent of adult children, it doesn't really mean that I am inadequate. It's just a feeling. I always remember that emotions come and go, they rise and fall. This too was another opportunity for me to ride the emotional roller-coaster. I have my seat belt on and I'm feeling safe and sound with my children's' stamp-of-approval. Yes, validation!

My experience with this emotion:

How did I manage this emotion?

How did I manage the social setting?

Lessons learned from this emotion:

If faced with this situation again, what would I do differently:

REFLECTIONS

REFLECTIONS

VULNERABLE

Vulnerable –"Capable of or susceptible to being wounded or hurt, as by a weapon; a vulnerable part of the body; open to moral attack, criticism, temptation, etc."

- Merriam-Webster's Dictionary

MY EXPERIENCE WITH THIS EMOTION:

If I could sum up my experience with being vulnerable, it could be summed up in one word, ah, maybe two - "This BOOK!" I know I've written about this experience under the emotion of fear, however, I felt like I had to write about it again.

Even though fear and vulnerable are two different emotions, they consistently show up as Siamese twins for me. I found it difficult to separate the one from the other, so I thought I'd try it again...Here we go! I've been working on this book for about a year now. There are two emotions that have held me back and they are FEAR and VULNERABLE.

There were so many times when I've sat down to write this book and I would stop, or not write for days or weeks. I would try to fool myself, (but not really) and say I'll write it next month, I will write this weekend. I'm the kind of person that when I make up my mind to do something, I will usually accomplish it. This book was set for an October 2018 launch and I was very disappointed when I had to push it back. When I allowed myself to sit in the silence and stare at these Siamese twins Fear and Vulnerable, some of the thoughts that ran through my mind were: "What if people don't like the book?" I've opened my heart, mind, and soul in this book, writing about my family, my children and my innermost emotions, definitely opening myself up to be judged, criticized and emotionally wounded. In this space, fear rises up and lodges in my chest and then quickly moves to my heart. I feel the pain there, then my heart starts beating faster. From these fearful thoughts, emotionally I'm weak, and physically my legs weaken so I just sit. However, I did not just experience this emotion just once — this space of being open and vulnerable was like an uninvited distant relative knocking on the door with her twin sister named FEAR. They would take up lodging for days, sometimes weeks and both brought their share of baggage.

HOW DID I MANAGE THIS EMOTION?

Initially, I allowed this emotion to control me. I wasted time pretending this emotion was something else like fatigue. "I'm too tired to write." Or a busy schedule. "I'm too busy to write." They were all just excuses that sound pretty good.

Eventually, this became the focus of discussion with my coach. It was in this session that I began to try and separate the Siamese twins. I could separate fear from vulnerable. What does it look like when I'm vulnerable? I'm open, kind, sharing and moving forward. "What does it look like when I'm fearful?" I'm stuck, stagnant and unproductive. I also began to think that in my daily life I'm very open with my feelings and thoughts, I'm comfortable in that space. In fact, my ability to be vulnerable is one of the things that makes a great facilitator. So, I asked myself, how is this any different? It is

because it has the potential to be heard on a much broader scale. However, in the moments when I told myself that I'm not going to write this book, the emotion to help others was greater than my fear of publicly being vulnerable. Here I am face-to-face with myself again.

I prayed about writing this book so many times. It seems like my answers came in every interaction I had with my coaching clients, in a training session I facilitated, even in the form of emails. Today, I received an email from a friend who said, "I'm tired of feeling inadequate." I thought, "WOW, I've written about this emotion in my book. I can't wait until she has an opportunity to explore this emotion in my book and journal on it."

I guess I managed this emotion by thinking about the good that could occur by helping others and not focusing so much on myself. I also thought about all of the times in the past that I've been vulnerable and how most often it creates a space for others to feel safe enough to share their real emotions. Being vulnerable gives others permission to do the same. I also think about experiences in the past where I've shared a piece of myself and I have felt judged, hurt and misunderstood, and yet here I am today. I am still in this space. There was nothing that happened to me in the past that I didn't overcome with resilience. This is my way of validating this emotion…the big V…Vulnerable.

HOW DID I MANAGE THE SOCIAL SETTING?

The social setting associated with this emotion was being able to talk this out with my coach. Being very vulnerable in this space. What I love about coaching is that it creates a space for the monologue in my head to have an external voice. Hearing myself talk out the emotion of being vulnerable helped me to separate my fears from reality. I was also empowered to distinguish the truth from the "story" I'd been telling myself. Once I felt the energy from being empowered, I was able to move forward and continue writing. If you're reading this book, I certainly overcame my fear of being vulnerable.

IF FACED WITH THIS SITUATION AGAIN, WHAT WOULD I DO DIFFERENTLY:

Come face-to-face with myself a lot sooner.

LESSONS LEARNED FROM THIS EMOTION:

Like any other emotion, this one has its place. I've learned to validate the fear of being vulnerable every time it bubbles up, however it doesn't have as much power. It's real and it has a purpose, but I don't have to succumb to the imagined power of this feeling. I love this quote from Nelson Mandela, "May your choices reflect your hopes, not your fears." My hope that others will benefit from this book, is greater than my fear of being hurt, judged or wounded. I intentionally chose to keep it moving!

My experience with this emotion:

How did I manage this emotion?

How did I manage the social setting?

Lessons learned from this emotion:

If faced with this situation again, what would I do differently:

REFLECTIONS

LIST OF EMOTIONS

Aggression
Amazed
Anger
Annoyed
Anxiety
Anxious
Apathy
Ashamed
Bitter
Boredom
Comfortable
Confused
Contempt
Content
Depression
Determined
Disdain
Disgusted
Doubt
Eager
Embarrassment
Empathy
Energetic
Envy
Euphoria
Fear
Foolish
Frustrated
Frustration
Furious
Gratitude
Grief
Grieving
Guilt
Happiness
Hatred
Hope
Hopeful
Horror
Hostility
Hunger
Hurt
Hysteria
Inadequate
Insecure
Inspired
Irritated
Jealous
Joy
Loneliness
Lonely
Lost
Love
Loving
Miserable
Motivated
Nervous
Overwhelmed
Paranoia
Peaceful
Pity
Pleasure
Pride
Proud
Rage
Regret
Relieved
Remorse
Resentful
Sadness
Satisfied
Scared
Self-Conscious
Shame
Shock
Shocked
Silly
Suffering
Surprise
Suspicious
Sympathy
Tense
Terrified
Trapped
Uncomfortable
Worried
Worthless

REFLECTIONS

REFLECTIONS

REFLECTIONS

REFLECTIONS

REFLECTIONS

REFLECTIONS

REFLECTIONS

Emotional Intelligence Leadership Training Questions

1. When have you experienced fear and/or intimidation in the workplace and how did it impact your performance?

2. Think about a time when you were in a situation at work and you could see beneath the surface as to what was really going on, you were insightful, how did this emotion help or hinder you?

3. How often do you feel grateful for your team members or your organization?

4. How do you express or demonstrate gratitude for your team? (Its one thing to feel it, it's another to demonstrate and express).

5. We are all gifted, have you discovered your natural gifts and talents?

6. What are your natural gifts and talents and how do you use them at work?

7. What would happen if you unleashed your natural gifts and talents?

8. When have you experienced the emotion of jealousy in the workplace, and how did it impact your relationships and/or performance?

9. What happens when you feel connected to your team? What impact does it have on your performance and your team's performance?

10. How often do you feel vulnerable at work, and what do you do with this emotion?

11. As a leader, what makes you happy?

12. What are some of the challenges you face as a leader that might make you feel defeated? How do you manage this emotion?

13. Think about a time when you were offended, what did you do with this emotion?

14. As a leader, what do you do when you are tired?

15. Think about a time when you have felt inadequate, how did that impact your performance and what did you do with this emotion?

16. Think about a time when you worked with a leader who made you feel squashed, how did this emotion impact your performance?

17. How did you handle the situation?

18. As a leader, has there been a time when you may have made members on your team feel squashed? What were the circumstances? What were you feeling on the inside that resulted in your behavior?

19. What have you taken away from this 30-day journey?

20. How will this experience help you in your role as a leader?

Book Club Questions

1. How many emotions in the book resonated with you?

2. Which emotion resonated with you the most?

3. How will listening to a particular emotion enhance your relationships?

4. Which emotion was the most difficult for you to sit with and write about?

5. Which emotions screamed the loudest for you?

6. Which emotion was the most difficult for you to validate?

7. Which emotion is the most difficult for you to manage and why?

8. What is the value of being able to name and articulate your emotions?

9. All emotions manifest themselves in the body, where did you physically feel your emotions?

10. Which stories do you think were written after I was able to manage my fear?

11. How has this book helped you?

12. How will this book help you in your personal/ professional life?

13. Who do you want to share your discoveries with?

14. At what age would you have liked to learn about emotional intelligence?

15. How would your life be different had you learned about emotional intelligence at that age, and what are some things you would have done differently?

Dear Reader:

Thank you from the bottom of my heart for bearing with me on this 30-day emotional Journey. "Whew!" I know it was "pretty deep" (as my husband always says), but if you made it this far, I'm sure it has proved to be worth the effort.

I hope you will cherish the pieces of my heart and soul that I have shared with you, so you, in turn, can honor, comfort, and validate all of the emotions you have intentionally taken time to explore.

I applaud you for the courage and dedication you have demonstrated as you purposefully created the time and space to Shh...Just Listen and allow great things to happen in the silence. I'm hoping this journal is just the beginning of a journey that has the potential to be transformational as you unlock the phenomenal person lying just beneath the surface of a plethora of unheard and maybe repressed emotions. Continue to empower yourself to listen and give voice to your emotions on your terms. While some emotions may be intense, don't let them hijack you. Remember, you can be intentional to respond to your emotions instead of reacting to them.

To assist you along the way, I've included additional journal pages and a list of just a few emotions to keep you on track with your newly-established routine. Yes, this 30 days was just a start to a "journey that may never end."

Transformation happens when we take time to, "Shh...Just Listen." Because Great Things Happen in the Silence.

~Cathy~

ABOUT THE AUTHOR

Cathy Mott is a Leadership & Life coach with a specialty in Social and Emotional Intelligence coaching. She has had the pleasure of training thousands and coaching hundreds on their journey to increase their level of emotional intelligence. She excels at creating a safe space for her clients to come face-to-face with themselves and explore their emotions on their terms instead of moving through life being emotionally highjacked. Inspired by her own personal journey to increasing her emotional intelligence and the work she has done in many organizations, Cathy has created this Emotional Intelligence Workbook, that will tug at your heart, challenge your intellect, and touch your soul and enlighten your spirit. In the midst of all of this, you will be invited to join Cathy on this journey of increasing your emotional intelligence and learning to recognize that we all have the ability to either react or respond to our emotions. Cathy has witnessed the truthfulness of Daniel Goleman's words, "Emotional Intelligence is four times more important in determining the success of an individual than Intellectual Intelligence." In 1998, in what has become one of HBR's most enduring articles, "What Makes a Leader," states unequivocally:

> The most effective leaders are all alike in one crucial way: they all have a high degree of what has come to be known as emotional intelligence. It's not that IQ and technical skills are irrelevant. They do matter, but...they are the entry-level requirements for executive positions. My research, along with other recent studies, clearly shows that emotional intelligence is the sine qua non of leadership. Without it, a person can have the best training in the world, an incisive, analytical mind, and an endless supply of smart ideas, but he still won't make a great leader.

With that in mind, Cathy has created a 30-day Emotional Intelligence Workbook, that goes out of the classroom setting and takes you to a place that you intentionally create to take this journey. This expedition takes courage, commitment and an open mind and heart. The best leaders are authentic, which means they show up as they truly are whether they are in the workplace or at home.

Through her personal and professional life experiences, it is Cathy's desire that you create a safe space in your life to take this transformational journey if you Shh...Just Listen and allow great things to happen in the silence.

CATHY MOTT, PCC, ISEI

CEO & President of CWC Leadership Development, LLC
www.cwcleadershipdevelopment.com
cathymott@cwcleadershipdevelopmentllc.com
PCC - International Coaching Federation
(Credentialed over 2500 hours of coaching)
ISEI - Institute of Social & Emotional Intelligence
(Certified EI Coach)

CERTIFICATIONS AND CREDENTIALS

- Leader as Coach – Bluepoint Leadership
- Social & Emotional Intelligence Co - ISEI
- PCC - Professional Certified Coach, International Coaching Federation (2500 Hours)
- Customer Experience Training – Starizon
- Change Leadership and Culture Change Professional
- CCL 360 Assessor, Centers for Creative Leadership
- Just Culture Facilitator, Outcome Ingenuity
- Crucial Conversations Certified Trainer, Vital Smarts
- Multi-Cultural Leadership – New Detroit
- Insights Discovery

Cathy Mott is available for the following:

to facilitate
Emotional Intelligence (EI) Training and
Coaching at your company or organization

to facilitate
a book club meeting for your group or organization

to work with you individually,
to provide you with an Emotional Intelligence
assessment and/or provide coaching

Cathy can be reached at **shhjustlisten2019@gmail.com**